DATE DUE

OPPORTUNITIES IN
LAW ENFORCEMENT
AND CRIMINAL JUSTICE

James D. Stinchcomb

VGM Career Horizons
A Division of National Textbook Company
4255 West Touhy Avenue
Lincolnwood, Illinois 60646-1975 U.S.A.

ABOUT THE AUTHOR

James D. Stinchcomb is presently the Director of the Southeast Florida Institute of Criminal Justice, the regional training center for all of Dade County (Miami) Florida. He was previously an Associate Professor in and Chairman of the Department of Administration of Justice and Public Safety at Virginia Commonwealth University. He has served in Washington, D.C. as the criminal justice staff director for a national consulting firm, and previous to that held a full-time consultant assignment with the U.S. Department of Justice under the Law Enforcement Assistance Administration's Law Enforcement Education Program (LEEP).

Previously, the author served on the staff of the American Association of Community and Junior Colleges (AACJC) under a Kellogg Foundation grant as specialist for public service education. He was training and education consultant for the International

---

1985 Printing

Copyright © 1984 by National Textbook Company
4255 West Touhy Avenue
Lincolnwood (Chicago), Illinois 60646-1975 U.S.A.
All rights reserved. No part of this book may
be reproduced, stored in a retrieval system, or
transmitted in any form or by any means, electronic,
mechanical, photocopying, recording or otherwise,
without the prior permission of National Textbook Company.
Manufactured in the United States of America.
Library of Congress Catalog Number: 84-60165

4 5 6 7 8 9 0 BB 9 8 7 6 5 4 3 2

Association of Chiefs of Police under a Ford Foundation grant. He chaired the Department of Police Administration at St. Petersburg (Florida) Junior College and developed the bachelor's degree program in law enforcement at Florida State University.

After completing a Bachelor of Science degree in psychology, Director Stinchcomb served in the Louisville, Kentucky Police Department. He holds a Master of Arts degree in criminology and completed all coursework in the criminology doctoral program at Florida State University. He is a lecturer in the Administration of Justice Program at the University of Pittsburgh and has served as a part-time faculty member at eight other community colleges and universities.

In his consulting capacity, the author has visited over 150 educational institutions to review and assess their efforts in law enforcement and criminal justice. He is the co-author of two AACJC publications—*Guidelines for Law Enforcement Education Programs in Community and Junior Colleges* and *Law Enforcement Training and the Community College.* In addition, he is volume editor of the J. G. Ferguson Publishing Company's *Career Opportunities: Community Service and Related Specialists* and is series editor for all Prentice-Hall criminal justice publications, including both textbooks and training manuals.

In recent years, Director Stinchcomb also has served as consultant to the President's Crime Commission on Law Enforcement, the National Sheriffs' Association, Westinghouse Justice Institute, Public Administration Service, and a number of state and local organizations. He was an original member of the grant review panel for the Law Enforcement Education Program under LEAA and served as project director for a U.S. Office of Education grant to develop a curriculum guide for law enforcement programs. Most recently, his major consultant role was as criminal justice education specialist to the National Planning Association in Washington, D.C. He also serves regularly as an accreditation team member for the American Council on Education in its program to evaluate law enforcement training within the military. Director Stinchcomb is the author of several articles and chapters in college textbooks on police issues.

FOREWORD

Law enforcement is a vocation that is striving to become a true profession. During the last twenty years significant steps have been taken by the law enforcement component in the total criminal justice complex of agencies to increase its efficiency, improve relations with the community, develop sets of professional standards, inaugurate higher levels of training and education, raise its overall image as a service agency, and create new and higher levels of recruitment and retention of qualified personnel.

Opportunities for individuals to enter law enforcement have been growing, whether at the local, state or national levels. However, many of the opportunities are obscure. For example, at various levels in law enforcement agencies civilian positions are increasing. The age of technological advances has made its impact in the law enforcement agency creating highly sought after skills that were unknown a decade ago. The availability of law enforcement openings for women has fostered new opportunities for a whole new group of persons.

Comparatively little has been published that concisely, accurately and relatively completely focuses attention on the opportunities available in law enforcement in particular and in the criminal justice system in general.

Professor Stinchcomb has written in concise and practical form a book devoted to the actual functions and requirements of personnel who operate within the complex of criminal justice agencies. He describes in some detail the opportunities at federal, state and local levels. He has in general provided a compact history of law enforcement that succinctly outlines the transition of police work from the

v

"watch and ward" system to the complexity of modern agencies having over 25,000 personnel responsible for huge geographical areas and populations. He describes precisely the qualifications and skills required with some emphasis devoted to increased educational requirements.

Professor Stinchcomb in this new edition has further expanded on the topics he addressed in the first. He has produced an excellent resource for those persons seeking to enter law enforcement or some other component in the criminal justice field and for those contemplating a change of careers. His knowledge of the administration of justice and law enforcement is evident.

George T. Felkenes, Chair
Department of Criminal Justice
Claremont Graduate School
Claremont, CA 91711

CONTENTS

Mounted police are used today in some major cities. Photo: NTC

CHAPTER 1

THE HISTORY AND SCOPE
OF LAW ENFORCEMENT

When one views the history of the American police establishment, it is clear that the system is a complex one which has emerged from circumstances that are not responsive to today's mobile and industrialized urban communities. Originally, the English system encouraged mutual responsibility and even was known as the "mutual pledge system." The term "hue and cry" became a familiar one as citizens were alerted to their personal responsibility for preservation of the peace. As time went on, the family grouping known as the "hundred" arose, and out of that era arose the constable, whose primary duties related to custody of horses and weapons. When several "hundreds" merged themselves into "shires," we had the office of Shire-Reeve emerging. This office was appointed by the crown, was largely responsible for keeping peace and order, and in it could, of course, be seen our modern term "sheriff."

In 1066, William the Conqueror invaded England. Most historians refer to this period as a critical one in legal developments. The philosophy of an enforcement unit separated from the judiciary evolved.

By the late 1200s, England had created a "watch and ward" system with concern for fire protection, guarding the town gate, and nighttime security. Gradually, the constable gained in acceptance, and for centuries he was to serve as "conservator" under the Justice of the Peace.

1

Gradually, the concept of assigning to land owners the responsibility of keeping the king's law gave way to taxation for the purpose of paying men who served as enforcers. In 1777, under King George II, wages were established from taxes, relieving merchants and land owners of the financial burden of law enforcement. Also, by this time, law enforcement had become a demanding task because of the pressures of the Industrial Revolution. The rural-to-urban migration which accompanied the Revolution and the mob violence which led to use of military force paved the way for legislation clearly identifying the civil police.

Many law enforcement experiments before 1820 failed because no system could reconcile individual freedom of action with the security of person and property. It remained for Sir Robert Peel, England's Home Secretary, in 1829 to introduce into the Parliament the Act for Improving the Police In and Near the Metropolis. This led to the first organized British metropolitan police force, structured along military lines and numbering 1,000 men. These "bobbies," despite low pay, recruitment problems, and resistance from Parliament, proved so effective that similar units were established throughout England, and by 1856, Parliament had provided for every borough and county to have a police force.

The Peelian Act of 140 years ago set forth principles which are still pertinent today, and they are set down here because they remain as basic tenets of the law enforcement profession:

- The police must be stable, efficient, and organized along military lines.
- The police must be under governmental control.
- The absence of crime will best prove the efficiency of police.
- The distribution of crime news is essential.
- The deployment of police strength, both by time and area, is essential.
- No quality is more indispensable to a policeman than a perfect command of temper; a quiet, determined manner has more effect than violent action.
- Good appearance commands respect.
- The securing and training of proper persons is at the root of efficiency.

- Public security demands that every police officer be given a number.
- Police headquarters should be centrally located and easily accessible.
- Police should be hired on a probationary basis.
- Police records are necessary to the correct distribution of police strength.

DEVELOPMENT IN AMERICA

American colonists in the seventeenth and eighteenth centuries brought to America the law enforcement structure with which they were familiar in England. The transfer of the offices of constable and sheriff to rural American areas—which included most colonial territory—was accomplished with little change in structure of the offices.

Generally speaking, the constable became responsible for law enforcement in the towns, while the sheriff took responsibility of the counties. Also, many colonial cities adopted the nightwatch system; Boston, as early as 1636, had nightwatchmen. The New York nightwatchmen were known as the "Rattlewatch," because they carried rattles on their rounds. Gradually, as in England, American cities began to develop their own police forces. Although Philadelphia established such a force in 1833, the oridinance was repealed several years later. In 1838, Boston created a day force to reinforce its nightwatch. In 1844, the New York legislature passed a law creating the first 24-hour organization, and, following that model, most major cities unified their day and night forces until by 1870, all cities had full-time police departments. During the remainder of the nineteenth century, a number of efforts were made to reform and improve policing both in the city and in the rural areas. Civil service enactment proved helpful, and some forces moved gradually to merit employment and less political interference. Police training schools emerged in the early 1900s, and, although quite modest, they set a goal which by mid-twentieth century had become generally accepted.

Noteworthy, of course, during the 1920s was the prophetic leadership of Chief August Vollmer at Berkeley, who advertised in the University of California's student newspaper for young men to serve on the police department while obtaining their college education. Vollmer's criteria for selection were simple and direct: "high intelligence, sound nerves, good physique, sterling character, fast reaction time, good memory, and the ability to make accurate observations and correct decisions."

MODERN TRENDS

In 1965, the International Association of Chiefs of Police Advisory Council on Police Education and Training, a group of national authorities assembled under a Ford Foundation Grant, stated that:

> . . . generally, it is conceded that today's law enforcement officer has a need for higher education. It is also generally agreed that within the next few years, law enforcement officers will find higher education imperative.

The above observation is the result of consideration of the changes that society has and is experiencing in such areas as the population explosion, the growing pressure for education beyond high school, the changing nature of metropolitan areas, and the effects of tensions and pressures ranging from automation to race. The law enforcement officer is required to meet all kinds of people and innumerable kinds of situations; he or she must therefore:

1. Be equipped to make good value judgements.
2. Be able to maintain one's perspective.
3. Be able to understand underlying causes of human behavior.
4. Be able to communicate clearly and precisely.
5. Possess leadership qualities and make decisions.

6. Be knowledgeable of skills.

In view of changing conditions which require flexibility, basic theory, and broad understandings, it is concluded that a wide spectrum of higher education must be available.

A published committee report from the International Association of Police Professors (now the Academy of Criminal Justice Sciences) that same year reads as follows:

> The transformation of the United States from a rural to an urban society, the tremendouse social problems resulting from herding people together in vast conglomerations around urban centers, the rapid acceleration of the drive for equality, the breakdown of many of our institutions which have heretofore maintained social stability, pose problems for police which are greater in both magnitude and complexity than those which they have faced before. We believe they demand changes in some of our approaches to police work. They require an increasing knowledge of the social sciences, especially psychology and sociology, and they require the capacity to adapt an array of technological devices to police work. Furthermore, it seems that at least the larger police departments of this country will not be able to escape the trend toward increasing specialization which is characteristic of virtually all other occupations in American society. This means that law enforcement education programs must be planned so that they will include a core of work in the law enforcement field for all law enforcement officers, plus the opportunity to develop special skills within this broad field.

The federal publication of the National Advisory Commission on Criminal Justice Standards and Goals (1973) again emphasized that college studies were essential to achieving professionalism. It specifically recommended that all police officers have an undergraduate degree no later than 1982. In the meantime, the standards proposed that all police officers should have at least two years of college for the present time, and three years of college by the 1980s.

While these optimistic timetables have not been met universally, there are many areas of the nation where it is not uncommon at all to find police academy's with a majority of recruits possessing at least two years of college.

POLICING IN AMERICA IN THE 1980s

The legal and procedural complexities have increased so greatly that police officers are expected to have a significant knowledge of court decisions regarding searches and seizures, inquiries, and arrests, along with the difficult burden of having to make those decisions on the spot and without benefit of analysis and discussion. Officers must also recognize and understand a body of professional knowledge that has emerged from sociology and psychology, but which is more appropriately referred to as Human Relations, Crisis Intervention, and Crisis Management.

Officers also note an increased need for them to become better generalists on a number of matters relating to safety and crime prevention that previously had not been demanded of all police officers.

On the other hand, the fields of technology have become more widespread in use and will have more impact upon policing than ever was imagined a few decades ago. This will result in the use of more scientific techniques to plot incidents and occurrences, to examine evidence, to collect and assess data, and to aid in predicting events. While instrumentation, computers, walkie-talkies, and other devices may influence results, the occupational involvement in the control and managing of these devices, as well as the interpretation of their outputs for effective action, will increase for street officers.

The hard issues of years gone by, such as the role of the police officer as crimefighter versus his role as a community service agent, may not be resolved in the 1980s; however, the challenge from the community will continue to be very real and extremely conflicting at times. The more one can become educated ahead of such a career, the better, although that alone will not resolve the dilemma created by a financially pinched community demanding better protection and greater crime prevention efforts from its police department.

Among the improvements which are underway throughout the police service are better management techniques, wider use of computer assistance, more attention to performance evaluations, and considerable attention to training needs.

The 1980s are witnessing full professional status for the police officer in America. Educational requirements, communication skills, technological support, and other attributes will enlarge his position and enhance his image considerably. It will always to recognized that the police officer is on the cutting edge of violence and disorder, and must possess the skills to confront these matters effectively. The physician must do this in meeting cases in an emergency room of a hospital; so must the police officer make wise decisions quickly and under much pressure.

To summarize then, the United States emerged patterned after the London and the English system and made little significant professional progress until the post-Civil War period. Gradually certain areas emerged as legal responsibilities of the states and others became solely federal government functions. The student of police history will want to review the Pendleton Act to better understand police administration and how reform began to take effect in the form of civil service systems.

The student of issues relating to citizen control, community crime-watch, and/or collective protection programs (even including the hiring of private forces) will surely want to review the writings on vigilante groups, and "how the West was won" by such famed legends as Hickok, Earp, and Masterson.

Watchers of the presidential commissions should become familiar with the 1929 Wickersham Commission appointed by President Hoover, and the more recent one appointed in 1967 by President Johnson. *The Challenge of Crime in a Free Society*, published along with a number of *Task Force Reports*, was the product of the *President's Commission on Law Enforcement and Administration of Justice.* Its many conclusions are very valuable contributions to the literature and led to the federal government's decision to distribute funds to assist in the control of crime. No one who really wants to understand the evolution of the police and the various situations that impact upon how the police operate can afford to ignore the writings that appear in these milestones of governmental documents.

It is interesting and quite revealing to note that professional literature, textbooks and journals are largely products of the last 40 years. Thus, in little more than a generation, a profession of law enforcement has arisen, assembled its history, assessed its own status, enacted standards, made national recommendations, and clearly set its goals to be consistent with the same demands that are made of other long established and recognized competent human endeavors.

PERSONNEL NEEDS

Few occupations in the public service field offer as challenging and varied a career as that of law enforcement. Whether at the federal, state, or local level, employment opportunities continue to grow because of population expansion and social complexities. Undoubtedly, the police of the world have emerged from a history of uncertainty as to their proper functions, but in the United States, as representatives of all citizens, they are responsible for maintaining peace and order within the frame work of the law. The police role is changing rapidly and is enjoying greater stature and prestige than ever before.

In years past, certain requirements for peace officers were not as rigid, and the service was not effectively competing for young persons with education. More recently, partly because of the community concern that has been expressed over crime and disorder, law enforcement finds itself on the threshold of professional status and its career appeal increasing. The urgency and importance of policing was described by the President's Commission on Law Enforcement and Administration of Justice in its special *Task Force Report* [on the] *Police*:

> The police . . . are the part of the criminal justice system that is in direct daily contact both with crime and with the public. The entire system—courts and corrections as well as the police—is charged with enforcing the law and maintaining order. What is distinctive about the responsibility of the police is that they are charged with performing these functions where all eyes are upon them and where the going is roughest, on the street.

By publication time of the National Advisory Commission on Criminal Justice Standards and Goals report in 1973, the police numbered nearly 600,000, of whom 60,000 worked at the federal level and 78,000 at the state level.

The police are by far the largest segment of the criminal justice system, when one realizes that there were just slightly over one million criminal justice employees nationally in 1973. That 600,000 personnel figure for police agencies was confirmed in 1976 by the National Manpower Study and the total of all employees was shown to be 1.1 million public justice workers. Nearly 200,000 were in the courts and legal services, and about 217,000 employed in corrections services and institutions. The administration of justice in the United States is overwhelmingly a function of local government. 81% of the more than 55,000 justice agencies are concentrated at the local level. There are, according to the U.S. Bureau of Justice Statistics, 13,414 general purpose police organizations, almost all at the municipal and township levels.

Some other data regarding law enforcement shows that there are 3028 county sheriff's departments, and that 83% of these sheriff's offices operate jails. In addition to the general purpose police, there are 1122 special police units. 55% of these are on the state level, including mostly college and university security agencies. The number of agencies will vary considerably from one state to another depending upon population and the units of government. When added together, nearly 20,000 state and local agencies are responsible for maintaining public order and enforcing the laws.

Local control over police is very much an American tradition, and over 90% of all municipalities with a population over 2500 receive police protection from their own agency; hence, the figure of 13,414. Close to two-thirds (63%) of all these municipal units have less than ten sworn officers.

There are recommendations and even movements to consolidate some of these smaller units, often through a contract with other larger communities or the sheriff's agency. In fact, in the past several years, the actual number of municipal police agencies has declined somewhat because of an increase in contractual arrangements, consolidation efforts and other attempts to streamline and economize the numbers of different organizations. Some of the non-municipal departments would be the county police agencies found in some states, housing and port authorities, townships, special districts and school districts. Even a park police may be a separate and special unit. In addition to the county sheriff's, there are 49 independent cities that have a sheriff because of a consolidated city-county form of government.

It should be noted too, that some County police departments are among the largest of any type police organizations; some of these are Los Angeles Sheriff with 5732 officers; Dade County (FL) with 2100 officers; Nassau County (NY) with 3318; Suffolk County (NY) with 2632 officers; and Baltimore County (MD) with 1377 officers.

Some examples of total sworn officers in major cities will demonstrate how large local police departments may be. New York City now has over 23,000 officers and has made recent proposals for increases in strength. Some cities, like New York, once had larger organizations but municipal budget tightening has resulted in personnel reductions. Chicago shows over 12,000 officers at this writing; Los Angeles has about 7000; Philadelphia over 7200; Detroit about 4000 officers and Houston has 3600. Those city departments staffing over 2000 include Washington, D.C. with 3800; Baltimore with 3000; Dallas with 2000, and Cleveland with 2100. Just under this 2000 officer figure, one finds Boston with 1900; San Francisco with 1900; St Louis with 1800; and Phoenix with 1700.

What figures such as these say to the young person seeking a career is that opportunities exist throughout the nation in police work, but greater numerical vacancies will be found in the larger cities and heavily populated suburban counties which often surround the large city.

Many people prefer working in the communities other than the very largest urban complexes. For them, the options, of course, are many. Middle range cities have police departments numbering in the many hundreds. For example, Cincinnati has 971 officers as of our latest data. New Orleans reports 1371 sworn officers during this time period and Jacksonville, Florida has 1263 sworn officers.

Since 1974, the average number of all law enforcement employees per 1000 citizens has increased only very slightly nationally. The *1977 Uniform Crime Report*, published by the FBI reflected a figure of 2.5. By the *1983 Uniform Crime Report* the national figure had grown to 2.6 full time employees per 1000 inhabitants. If one considers only the figure for sworn law enforcement officers, not all employees, there were 2.0 full time officers employed per 1000 inhabitants in the nation as of the 1983 data. As these figures are further analyzed, the reader discovers that large cities have larger ratios of police employees to citizens than do the smaller communities. The range shows 2.7 sworn officers for cities over 250,000 population, and only 1.5 sworn for sheriff's departments or county police.

Furthermore, it should also be understood that civilian employment within law enforcement has been increasing. In 1973 civilians made up 14.6 percent of all police personnel and in 1977 that figure had increased to 17.5 percent civilians. In the *1983 Uniform Crime Report* the civilian figure had reached 19 percent for cities, further indicating that the trend to utilize more civilians continues. Many of these personnel are assigned to records, to communication units, to labs, to computers and planning work. In general, this suggests greater effort at productivity by moving non-enforcement duties away from sworn officers. The message seems clear that one might consider working for a police department, but in a civilian capacity. For the rural law enforcement agencies, the civilian figure is 27 percent, again demonstrating a strong commitment to civilianize much of the work of our suburban police.

Nationwide, the 1983 data indicated that female police officers have increased to 6 percent up from the 2 and 3 percent figures of recent decades.

In certain large cities, where the strong employment efforts have been concentrated, the hiring of female officers will be much greater. Female officers are really not new; they were hired in Los Angeles in 1910 for patrol work involving women and children. Major changes began to occur during the late 1960s and early 1970s when Washington D.C. became one of the first to employ patrolwomen in large numbers and in similar duties as men. However, although in limited numbers compared to men, it would be important to note that many communities did have police officers who were women during the 1930-1960 era. To be sure, many had specialized assignments dealing with crime prevention and delinquency matters, (although it was not uncommon for women to be given duties involving the investigation of crimes affecting the community well being). Nonetheless, no longer do female duty assignments occur only in communications, dispatching, clerical, records, property rooms or as jail matrons. They are now found in patrol cars more and more, and gradually in supervisory and command ranks as well. The National Sheriff's Association reports that there are now 11 female sheriffs in the country.

We said earlier that the overall percentage of women in policing has increased to 6 percent nationally; there are cities where the figure is much higher because they have sought to employ women over a period of time and have distributed assignments on an equitable basis. Some of the noteworthy cities in this regard are Washington D.C.; Miami, Florida; New York City; Atlanta, Georgia; Indianapolis, Indiana; and Detroit, Michigan.

Again, as with employment generally, chances for women in police work are greatest in the largest cities. In 1983 the percentage of female officers in cities over one million in population was 6.1%; in cities of half million up to one million there were 7% female officers. As one looks to the smaller cities and small towns this figure decreases to around 3%, but interestingly, increases again for rural and suburban counties, reflecting opportunities in county police and sheriff's departments. It should be pointed out too for those not interested in sworn positions that the female employment percentages in all agencies for civilian jobs are higher and significantly so.

In future chapters, the reader will find information about careers other than at the local level. Data now indicate that about 15% of military police officers are female. Likewise, agencies such as the FBI and the Secret Service have recruited women for over a decade now. The earliest state police units to recruit women include Pennsylvania and Maryland. The author highly recommends that young women interested in police careers seek out and speak with those who have achieved this career goal. *Breaking & Entering; Policewomen on Patrol* is a book highly recommended for those who may wish to locate a very detailed study of this subject.*

FUTURE OUTLOOK

New appointments must continue as estimates consistently place the number of entry level positions available at 30,000. Some others view this as a conservative estimate based upon traditional population and economic growth projections. The rise in crime and the public and political concern for public safety as the population grows and moves will always dictate a positive employment situation for jobs in police work. Retirements of those who entered in the post World War II period are now occuring and likewise, those with Korean conflict duty have now served thirty years. Projections of slower crime rate, governmental budget tightening, and reduced population expansion must be met with the turnover and the demands for new services. *The National Manpower Study*, conducted by the National Planning Association in Washington D.C. during the late 1970s indicated that police agencies would continue to grow in state, county, and suburban areas.

The United States Department of Labor's *Occupational Outlook*

Breaking & Entering; Policewomen on Patrol, Susan E. Martin. University of California, Berkeley Press, 1980, Paperback 1982.

Handbook states that the kinds of police jobs that arise in the future are likely to be affected to a considerable degree by the changes now taking place in enforcement methods and equipment. Specialists are becoming more and more essential, and there will be a greater need for officers with training ranging from engineering techniques applied to traffic control to social work techniques applied to crime prevention. Furthermore, as statistical analysis and data utilization increase, there are expanding needs for computer technicians, data analysts, and long-range planners. In addition, such new concepts as the *state specialist*, recommended by the National Advisory Commission on Criminal Justice Standards and Goals, will enhance career opportunities in this field. Several states already have developed state investigative specialty programs to assist local law enforcement agencies with crimes that require special investigative knowledge. The majority of these programs have been implemented for such specific problems as organized crime or consumer protection violations.

In summary, law enforcement is one of the largest of the career groups dealing in the public service. Because of our system of government, opportunities exist throughout all jurisdictions. At the federal level, our national government employs many thousands of investigative agents and specialists in departments such as Justice, Treasury, and Defense. The fifty states employ both civilian and sworn personnel in agencies known as either state police or highway patrols. At the local government level, where the vast number of career opportunities exist, there are sheriff's departments and municipal police agencies. Some areas of the country also have county police departments, and many communities employ township and borough police.

In the years ahead, much greater public attention will be called to police tasks that require considerable professional skills. To date, the many challenges facing law enforcement have not been apparent and have been little understood by the public. Police status and pay have increased significantly and educational achievements have been remarkable. Probably no single career group in history has ever achieved so much higher education in so short a time period as has the American law enforcement officer.

Many enforcement functions and duties cannot change overnight because the primary concern of the police is to protect the public. The police department is the 24-hour agency best equipped to respond to requests for aid. Nonetheless, many dramatic changes in assignments and procedures have occurred in recent years, and authorities generally agree that the role of the police in the American society is moving rapidly toward closer involvement in community-based programs, with greater emphasis on crime prevention and the reduction of hazards. Quite recently, the police have become particularly active in efforts aimed at specific offense reduction through programs to harden frequent targets, encourage greater use of locks and alarms, advise homeowners and the business community about crime risks, and, in general, become more aggressive in reducing the potential of crime dangers to the public. As events unfold in the years ahead, the enforcement officer must display greater insights into community problems, social sciences, and the complex factors that contribute to unlawful activities.

No one can predict entirely to what extent policing will change as more data become computerized and the agencies become more involved with community planning and crime prevention. It is safe to assume, however, that competent personnel will be in demand and that training and education have become an integral part of the system. Duties will correspond to those in other professions wherein job descriptions reflect a variety of tasks according to the level of career preparation. At that point, status and salary will be well beyond our estimates today. Also, at that point, policing will be acknowledged as deserving of full professional recognition, with rigid state licensing for those who practice its calling.

Much attention has been focused upon the police officer in America and the tremendous task of maintaining order. A great deal is being researched and written currently about the role of the police, but there is little doubt that the police perform one of the most essential, and often one of the least appreciated, services that exist anywhere. Few can dispute the importance of the men and women who must enforce our laws, prevent disorders, investigate offenses, and keep the peace. Without their efforts and constant vigilance, the daily routine of all of us would be in jeopardy, and through their continuous presence, most of us live the greater part of our lives free from attack or theft.

Despite frequent pressures and frustrations, the police service offers career opportunities unmatched in other vocations for those young persons who prefer working with a variety of circumstances in an unpredictable and changeable environment. The demands of the job are great; there are stresses and temptations, long hours and interrupted plans; weekends are just more work days; and many shifts end with the officer feeling unable to maintain order for eight hours in even one patrol area. This knowledge could affect work efficiency, so it is important that the applicant for such a career accept the realities of dealing with human problems. He or she must be able to accomplish the duties with emotional resilience. Consider the comments of a prominent psychologist who has studied police officers and their behavior:

> Reviewing the tasks we expect of our law enforcement officers, it is my impression that their complexity is perhaps greater than that of any other profession. On the one hand, we expect our law enforcement officer to possess the nurturing, cartaking, sympathetic, empathic, gentle characteristics of physician, nurse, teacher, and social worker as he deals with school traffic, acute illness and injury, juvenile delinquency, suicidal threats, and missing persons. On the other hand, we expect him to command respect, demonstrate courage, control hostile impulses, and meet great physical hazard. . . . He is to control crowds, prevent riots, apprehend criminals, and chase after speeding vehicles. I can think of no other profession which constantly demands such seemingly opposite characteristics.*

Law enforcement is one of the largest of the semiprofessional occupational groups. It is striving for professional status, and as the more progressive agencies continue to contribute new achievements,

---

*Dr. Ruth Levy, Peace Officers Research Project, National Institute of Mental Health Grant, San Jose, California.

the opportunities for greater service expand. As one noted authority on criminal justice sees the future:

> More police will be employed to keep pace with society. Professionalism will increase through greater stress on training. The trend toward more highly educated officers is inevitable. In order to accomplish this, higher pay scales will develop in a highly competitive job market. The criteria for selection will be modified to take advantage of evolving techniques that will measure more accurately the potential of candidates for law enforcement work. . . .
>
> More electronic equipment will be utilized. . . . New technology also will aid in solution of problems of police deployment.
>
> . . . there will certainly be more sharing of such personnel as burglary, arson, and homicide specialists. Training, communications, records, criminal laboratories, and correctional institutions will be increasingly specialized and merged to create greater overall efficiency.*

The career aspirant must recognize that law enforcement is not a single job or one particular assignment. The field encompasses a broad spectrum of functions and cannot be described as one in which certain characteristics are essential and others unimportant. The need for police professionals is extremely great; the opportunities for capable young people are unlimited. A new service has emerged in which police enjoy greater respect and status. Few careers can be more satisfying in terms of helping one's fellow human beings, and none offers a more exciting challenge.

---

*George T. Felkenes, *The Criminal Justice System: Its Functions and Personnel* (Englewood Cliffs, N.J.: Prentice-Hall, 1973), pp. 35-36.

Police officers assemble before going on patrol. Photo: San Francisco Police Department.

CHAPTER 2

OPPORTUNITIES AT THE
CITY AND COUNTY LEVELS

Counseling for a career choice in law enforcement varies rather extensively, depending upon the jurisdictional level which one expresses an interest in joining. The federal agencies are easier to apply for, in the sense that a single office furnishes information and applications and affords the applicant centralized procedural steps. Likewise at the state level, whether it be a state police or a highway patrol, there would be a central headquarters responsible for all personnel matters. It is at the local level, which is, of course, where the greatest number of opportunities exist, where no one procedure or process is available. Once an individual has made the decision to seriously consider entering this exciting and challenging field, contact should be made with the department in which the applicant is interested in order to obtain its specific requirements. However, this book will attempt to describe the entrance process generally found throughout city and county police agencies.

PERSONAL REQUIREMENTS

The process initially involves making formal written application to the agency on a form specifically furnished for that purpose. In addition to the questions about oneself, there will also appear questions regarding relatives, personal and business references, military service, and formal schooling. Quite possibly, the applicant will also be asked to state reasons for being interested in a law enforcement career with that particular organization. Naturally, United States citizenship is required by all law enforcement agencies. A large number of departments have eliminated prior residency requirements of the police applicant, although by no means have they been totally removed. State residency may be required prior to employment, but the trend now is to invite applications from any area of the United States. Once hired, an employee may be required to reside within a given city or county.

In the United States, entrance age requirements now range from a minimum of 21 (in some jurisdictions, 19), to a maximum of 29 years, although some departments may hire applicants up until ages 32 or 34. In certain circumstances, high school graduates may obtain employment through a cadet program. The cadet program allows individuals to be employed prior to reaching their twenty-first birthday, and it also provides for consideration of employment as a police officer upon reaching the twenty-first birthday. As discussed in another section of this book, cadet programs have enabled young persons to become acquainted with the police field through various nonenforcement tasks. An applicant might consider making formal application prior to age 21, as the process itself takes some time, and there are departments which permit the submission of applications as much as one year in advance. Also, there are departments which allow entrance into the training program if the recruit will become 21 years old at some date while training is in progress. Several major departments, notably Miami, Houston, Dallas, and Philadelphia, some years ago began to accept candidates under the age of 21, even authorizing them for street duty. It is to be expected that this recruiting procedure may well continue to expand. Also, as lateral transfers continue, there will be more opportunity to enter one department up to age 40 when the applicant has had prior police experience elsewhere.

All police departments require applicants to be of good moral character, emotionally stable, and mature. A serious criminal record, particularly conviction, will be the basis for rejection. Serious prior traffic violations, especially as an adult, could also result in disqualification, since possession of a valid motor vehicle operator's license is required. All applicants are given a thorough background investigation which will determine their integrity, reliability, and sobriety. The applicant's habits, conduct, and reputation in the community will be evaluated. Additional screening may also include one or a series of psychological tests, with or without accompanying interviews. Some police departments utilize psychiatrists to test and interview applicants, but this has proven costly and no more effective than psychological assessments. A polygraph examination may be required, and a personal interview is a certainty.

SELECTION REQUIREMENTS

Traditional selection criteria currently are being examined in light of concerns for equal opportunity. Much of the controversy came to light after research indicated that minority group members had difficulty in written test situations and in meeting what were claimed to be arbitrary physical requirements. Responsibility for police personnel procedures, especially selection practices, is shared frequently by a civil service or merit system and the police department. At the present time, a number of cooperative arrangements are under way to develop more universally effective procedures for selection.

In 1971, a national study conducted by the International Association of Chiefs of Police reported great variations in requirements. This data would indicate that differences in opinions exist, and little had been proven in the past regarding pre-employment standards and their relation to later career success. Although there are jurisdictional variations, it may be that a standard system encompassing selection, recruit training, and probationary field performance eventually will prove acceptable.

The most recent document prepared on police selection is *Police Personnel Practices in State and Local Governments* by the International Association of Chiefs of Police. This publication describes personnel management trends, as agencies respond to changing employment conditions and job requirements, and includes specific discussions on employment of female and minority personnel, recruitment, performance appraisal, and lateral transfer. Communities and personnel departments now may contract with firms for written tests that are valid and non-discriminatory.

WRITTEN TESTS

Written tests are common and practical, since they can be easily administered and scored and are very economical.* However, because written entry tests are being challenged currently, the most that can be said is that extensive research now is being conducted to determine the relevance of such tests. However, as alterations to conform with job analyses make them more valid and acceptable, written tests will doubtless be continued. Regardless of the type of written test the applicant may encounter, the following skills and traits will always assist in expressing oneself in writing: reading comprehension, analytical ability, self-expression, and capacity to retain details, recall events, and make decisions based upon facts.

All departments now require successful completion of high school, although various alternatives do exist, such as certification through the Armed Services Institute or equivalency examinations (GED) by a state department of education. Applicants are not generally required to be knowledgeable of law enforcement information prior to their employment, but an applicant possessing advanced academic knowledge in the field may reasonably be expected to be better qualified for such employment.

PHYSICAL EXAMINATIONS

Police service at any level of government requires physically sound personnel. Severe physical exertion is called for occasionally, and the applicant, male or female, must possess the stamina to

---

*The Public Personnel Association's *Police Officer Test* is frequently used for the written entrance exam.

work for long periods of time without rest.

Minimum medical standards have been established and observed by most departments. Generally, any marked deformity, overweight condition, or weak muscular development may result in disqualification. Hearing and visual acuity must be within acceptable limits, although most departments permit corrective lenses to be worn. Thus far, the courts have paid little attention to standards related to vision and general physical health, since these would appear to be reasonably job-related. Generally speaking, eyesight must be correctible to 20/20 and no color blindness.

Minimum height and weight requirements had become the subject of controversy, and height and weight standards are being made more flexible in order to include a more representative group of applicants. Again, however, solutions to such matters will remain, to a great extent, related to the prevailing medical examination, in order that weight be in proportion to height. But the minimum height standard clearly has been lowered.

Of course, anyone seeking a police appointment must undergo a complete clinical appraisal conducted through a medical examination. This often is requested early in the process, since certain physical conditions do account for a significant number of rejections. Blood pressure, heart conditions, lack of required strength and agility, and inadequate coordination skills can all result in medical rejection. Furthermore, recent evidence of drug usage will disqualify the applicant.

Certain physical agility requirements do appear to relate to the enforcement occupation, but rather than the more traditional skills appraised through exercise-type tests, research now is attempting to determine what kinds of physical skills are essential to the job. Some most likely to be retained will have to do with lifting and arm strength, the ability to drive a car, fire a weapon, disarm an assailant, and even swim. While physical agility tests may continue to vary throughout the country, their presence indicates that many physicians and civil service boards believe that a police applicant should be able to perform rigorous physical activities at an average or even above average level, and mere evidence of good health will not be sufficient for employment.

PERSONAL INTERVIEW

One almost unanimous requirement among enforcement agencies is some form of personal interview, and this can be of great importance. The interview board generally consists of several representatives from the police department, as well as someone from the personnel department of the employing jurisdiction. Interview lengths vary considerably, but the questions tend to revolve around the applicant's past work experience, education, personal history and characteristics, and reasons for choosing police work as a career. An applicant should bear in mind that the board will not only be judging responses to questions, but also personal appearance and manner. Of particular importance will be the applicant's expression of interest in a police career and intention to pursue it in a dedicated way.

Quite understandably, all police agencies require that a character or background investigation be conducted on each applicant. This is a time-consuming and costly procedure and almost always occurs toward the end of the selection process. Thus, this effort would not be expended on those applicants who had failed to qualify on previous criteria. It is important that the candidate furnish as much detail as possible so this investigation can be performed without unnecessary delays. As an example, complete names, titles, addresses, and phone numbers of references should be furnished. All previous employment and residence locations must be accurate, and an applicant should remember that he or she is being evaluated by the very information furnished. Failure to include all pertinent data or failure to account for time periods may be cause for serious delay and even rejection. If an applicant spent time in the military or in college, and there are brief time intervals when neither was the primary activity, the time gap should be accounted for.

In the event that the reader believes the application process is one which is appealing, and that he or she can successfully respond to the rather stringent requirements, then a law enforcement career may be for you. But before we leave the characteristics, expectations, and requirements outlined over the past few pages, let us again discuss and clarify those abilities which research has not established as critical to the tasks identified as applicable to these positions.

Whether they are reviewed, measured, examined, and reported through written exams, personal and group interviews, medical analyses, psychological screening, polygraph tests, assessment center exercises, psychiatric interviews, and/or agility and motor ability demonstrations, these traits have survived the research, and must be possessed by the applicant:

Directing Others. Initiate action, independently assume control of a situation; obtain information from others; direct, assist and provide guidance to others.

Interpersonal. Display courtesy and consideration for the problems, needs, and feelings of others in a fair manner; use discretion in exercising police authority.

Perception. Identify and understand the critical elements of a situation; observe situational details and conditions; recognize discrepancies or circumstances that require action; interpret the implications of such actions.

Decision Making. Use logical and sound judgment when responding to a situation based upon a recognition and understanding of the facts available; define problem situations and initiate actions based upon established guidelines and procedures.

Decisiveness. Willingly take action and make decisions based upon situational need; render judgments; willingly defend actions or decisions when confronted by others.

Adaptability. Being flexible when dealing with situations involving change; appropriately modify a course of action based upon changes in the situation; maintain constructive behavior despite time pressures, or pressures exerted by others.

Oral Communications. Clearly express oneself through oral means; property use grammar, vocabulary, eye contact, and voice inflection.

Written Communications. Clearly and effectively communicate relevant information through written means, use of accurate vocabulary, and proper grammar and spelling.

The above described characteristics are the result of the research conducted at the Dade-Miami (Florida) Assessment Center for entry level police officers, which identified and grouped 102 specific knowledge, skills, and abilities required of the entry-level police officer. Similar research has been conducted under Project Star (System Training & Analysis of Requirements for Criminal Justice Participants) over a period of three years in four states; (California, Texas, Michigan, and New Jersey). Further findings regarding job task analysis were reported by the National Planning Association (Washington D.C.) during its National Manpower Survey. These two major federally funded studies were produced during the period 1971-1976 and represented the most extensive review of personnel selection and training ever presented to this field. Students of criminal justice interested in matters relating to manpower development would be well advised to obtain these reports from college or agency libraries.

PROBATION, TENURE, AND PROMOTION

The length of the probation period after employment is usually one year, and two years at the most. After serving the probationary period successfully, the majority of departments assure job security, except for cases in which formal charges are brought against the employee.

Very few differences exist among most law enforcement agencies with regard to promotion. Likewise, most agencies do have a stated, formalized promotion program. Generally, seniority in a particular rank stands among those items considered in promoting an employee. An oral interview also is conducted, along with an evaluation of general service experience in the department. In addition, to attain most ranks, there may well be a written examination and some type of job performance assessment. Formal performance appraisals will be conducted as often as every month, or at least quarterly. Even if such personnel activity evaluations are only semi-annual, they provide valuable insights about an individual's ability to do the job.

Performance evaluations typically review the officer's levels as measured by a number of events.

These might include arrests, court convictions, persons interviewed in the course of patrol duties, cases investigated, reports filed, and numerous other categories. Any citizen complaints formally charged against the officer, and likewise, any commendations would also be considered. So might attitude, appearance, and professional demeanor.

In recent years, articulate, better-educated officers have done exceptionally well in front of the oral interview board, and promotions may well continue to occur in this manner until higher education becomes an inegral part of the requirements for promotion. In some of the more progressive agencies, there are now Assessment Centers in operation whereby simulated exercises, role playing, and objective reviews are conducted which assist in the promotional process. They do not necessarily replace written examinations or oral interviews, but they are a very useful method for making impartial comparisons among candidates for a position, and they are based upon actual behavioral events, and not just test scores. To the extent that the simulations are designed to resemble actual job demands and expectations, the Assessment Center may become the process for the future in selecting finalists for promotions in rank.

THE PATROL OFFICER

Who is the police patrol officer? What tasks are performed, and what skills must one have? Again, to quote from the President's Commission on Law Enforcement and Administration of Justice in the special *Task Force Report on the Police*:

> The heart of the police effort against crime is patrol—moving on foot or by vehicle around an assigned area, stopping to check buildings, to survey possible incidents, to question suspicious persons, or simply to converse with residents who may provide intelligence as to occurrences in the neighborhood.

The object of patrol is to disperse police in a way that will eliminate or reduce the opportunity for misconduct and to increase the likelihood that a criminal will be apprehended while he is committing a crime or immediately therafter. The strong likelihood of apprehension will presumably have a strong deterrent effect on potential criminals. The fact of apprehension can lead to the rehabilitation of a criminal, or at least to his removal for a time from the opportunity to break the law.

When patrol fails to prevent a crime or apprehend a criminal, the police must resort to investigation. Some investigation is carried out by patrol officers, but the principal responsibility rests with detectives. Investigation aims at identifying offenders through questioning victims, suspects, witnesses and others, through confronting arrested suspects with victims or witnesses, through photographs, or less frequently, through fingerprints or other laboratory analysis of evidence fround at crime scenes.

Patrol stands very high in police management's list of priorities, since most departments spend 90 percent of their budget for personnel and as much as 60 percent of their budget on patrol personnel specifically. Further strengthening the significance of patrol, the National Advisory Commission on Standard and Goals has recommended that every police administrator ensure maximum efficiency in the delivery of patrol services, including immediate response to incidents, an emphasis on the need for preventive patrol to reduce the opportunity for criminal activity, and the placement of a priority upon each request for police service.

Not only is patrol the backbone of the crime prevention effort, but is also the foundation of the greatest part of all community contact and communication. The patrol officer is the everyday representative of the law enforcement agencies to the community at large and has the greatest impact upon community life.

The International Association of Chiefs of Police developed the following job description for the police patrol officer.*

---

*Norman C. Kassoff, *Police Chief Magazine*, August, 1965.

General Duties

Is responsible through the enforcement of laws and ordinances for the protection of life and property in an assigned area during a specific period. Performs routine police assignments received from officers of superior ranks; conducts preliminary investigations; assists in the apprehension of criminals. Also performs special assignments requiring specialized skills or abilities.

Distinguishing Features of the Class

This work consists primarily of routine patrol tasks. Work may involve elements of danger and does involve many emergencies which demand that the employee must be able to exercise sound judgment and act without direct supervision. However, procedures and special assignments are usually carried out under immediate supervision.

Illustrative Examples of Work

Patrols a specific area in a patrol car, to preserve law and order, to prevent and discover the commission of crime, and to enforce parking and traffic regulations. Required to make close inspection of actual or potential hazards to the public safety.

Responds to complaints concerning automobile accidents, robberies, and other minor and major violations of law.

Interviews persons making complaints and inquiries and attempts to make proper disposition or direct them to proper authorities.

Investigates suspicious activities and makes arrests for violations of federal and state laws and local ordinances.

Watches for and makes investigations of wanted and missing persons and stolen cars and property.

Conducts preliminary investigations.

Administers first aid at the scenes of accidents and crimes.

Maintains order in crowds.

Answers questions and directs the public.

Performs periodic safety and crime prevention tasks as community requirements dictate.

Insures the rights of all citizens are protected and intervenes in disputes and disturbances to reduce their risk of becoming a crisis.

Required Knowledges, Skills, and Abilities

Good general intelligence and emotional stability.

Good judgment.

Ability to analyze situations quickly and objectively and to determine the necessary and proper action.

Ability to understand and carry out complex oral and written directions.

Good powers of observation and memory.

Ability to compose and legibly write or print complete factual reports.

A good knowledge of first aid methods, after training.

Ability to speak effectively.

Ability to drive a car.

Excellent moral character.

Excellent physical condition.

Physical strength and agility.

Skill in the use and handling of firearms, after training.

Let us look into this job description in detail and discuss just what it is that the police officer does. We cannot describe all of the assignments, but some common experiences are presented. It should also be noted that although the job information was written in the late 1960's, it is accurate and provides some assurance that the police service does not change the basic duties to be performed.

As indicated in the President's Commission on Law Enforcement and Administration of Justice in the special *Task Force Report* (on the) *Police*, an officer patrols a particular area or neighborhood, on foot or by vehicle. While on patrol, safe response to calls for assistance from the general public is a primary responsibility. These be initiated from police headquarters or directly by a citizen. In either case, what the police officer actually does after arriving at the scene largely depends upon what has happened.

First, the officer may find it necessary to hear a report from the victim of a crime or accident or from witnesses who observed the incident. The next course of action may require placing someone under arrest, or merely entering the information obtained into a report for later investigation. Depending on the situation involved, the patrol officer may be called upon at that moment to preserve the peace through some immediate action, or observe some piece of evidence that must be preserved and recorded. If an arrest is made, the suspect must be transported to the police station for the booking process. Enforcement personnel also assist the injured citizen in making a formal complaint. In the more serious cases, duties will include not only protecting the scene of the crime and obtaining information from witnesses, but also telling the detectives how the crime occured and giving them any available clues.

In the case of an accident, the police officer's duties involve rendering first aid, calling for an ambulance, preventing further damage, noting all pertinent facts, and obtaining statements from those involved as well as any witnesses. Of course, all of these matters necessitate a detailed recording and reporting of events.

The officer must also provide assistance in times of emergency whether the event be fire, catastrophe, rescue, or whatever. Police assistance is not only sought during major calamities; it may consist of hundreds of requests for services referred to only as miscellaneous: a domestic animal in trouble, a citizen in some distress, a lost child or elderly person, or such lost property as a bicycle, purse, or pet.

Often the police officer finds it necessary to issue traffic citations according to the motor vehicle code in the locale. Some violations may demand physical arrests, and, again, all will require full reporting of the action taken.

A great deal of time is devoted to observing and noting circumstances which could lead to more serious situations. Here the officer must identify *potential* hazards, whether they be neglect of children, the breeding of locations of vice, dangers to the personal safety of citizens, or any other conditions that might erupt into disorder or violence. Business locations also are inspected to reduce the likelihood of burglaries.

As one can readily see, little time is spent by police in the actual process of making arrests, but once an arrest is made, it is necessary for the officer to appear in the courtroom. This calls for preparing notes and testimony that are accurate and relevant to the case. The officer must repeat conversations accurately and introduce exhibits and evidence in such a manner that everyone is assured of one's professional competence.

One of the most sensitive of the tasks which must be performed is, of course, the use of physical force to restrain someone who may assault an officer or another citizen. The patrol officer must always be prepared to repel violent assaults by proficiency in defensive tactics or the use of weapons and must stay alert to prevent the escape of persons in custody.

In summary, when patrol officers are not engaged in riding patrol, answering emergency calls, handling citizen compalints, obtaining preliminary investigation information, making arrests, writing traffic citations and reports, or giving testimony in court, they are called upon by direct citizen contact on the street to deliver a variety of other services. Even beyond these duties, the officer will initiate action, upon individual judgment, without any direction from headquarters or other outside sources.

Automobiles are standard equipment for most police patrols in our country. A single uniformed officer in a marked patrol car is a familiar sight to everyone. Some circumstances demand that two officers ride patrol together, and communities generally find a combination of one-and two-officer vehicles to be the most appropriate policy. Few state police or deputy sheriffs patrol in pairs, but municipal officers handling numerous drunk or fight calls find it advantageous.

In recent years, the motorized scooter has become useful in traffic work because it places the police officer at the scene rapidly, unhampered by street congestion. Equipped with a walkie-talkie radio, the officer on a scooter is frequently in a position to confront a holdup or assault in progress.

Naturally, all of these methods may be used in varying degrees, depending upon the size of the community and demands made upon the department. A person choosing a police career can expect to spend much time in automobile patrol, but alternatives do exist. Flexibility is essential in delivering services to the public, and this variation has great appeal to most young persons. In helicopters, in patrol boats, sometimes working with canine units, and occasionally still on horseback, patrol officers pursue their missions of enforcing laws, protecting citizens and their property, preventing crime and disorder, and ensuring the peace.

A police career aspirant should bear in mind that the daily work schedule will differ somewhat from that of neighbors and friends. It must be recognized that patrol is a 24-hour-a-day activity and that it cannot be reduced on holidays or weekends, and, further, that many serious occurrences arise in the late evening and early morning hours. Beyond this, it must also be remembered that, because an officer is always a sworn protector of law and order, on-duty status is never really deserted. One is subject to call to duty at any time, to overtime and extended shifts, and most enforcement personnel must devote a large amount of their own time to completing the necessary reports and appearing in court.

Thus, a tour of duty on patrol may close without headlines and may, in fact, be relatively routine, but to the officer it may include hidden dangers, suspense, tedious monotony, and a few moments of tension and excitement. An unpredictable time, such as a quiet Sunday morning, can bring holdup and homicide.

As we observed earlier, few major changes or alterations have really occurred in the basic patrol functions in modern times; technology has improved, record systems are rapid, and the training available to officers has increased immensely. But patrol still entails covering one's assigned area, preventing crime, and providing service. Officers today are more aware of constitutional rights, legitimate dissent, and the implications upon taking official action, but fundamental responsibilities have not changed.

Body armor has been introduced, vehicles are safer and more efficient, mini-computers can now report back answers to field officers, and today's average police officer enjoys some distinct personal advantages in salary progression, benefits and support. Nonetheless, the job still demands intensity and alertness, and one continues to find that crime-fighting duties consume far less actual time than do the service and protection functions that occupy one's normal working hours.

However, one notable and significant change that deserves comment has been the steadily increasing numbers of women on patrol. In another section of this book, it is pointed out that the number of female officers has grown from 2-3% of sworn officers during the 1960-77 time period, to about 6% currently. Probably even more importantly, the duties have expanded from the original ones of dealing with delinquents, youth, female offenders, and staff support assignments, to the full array of patrol and investigative functions.

Going back nearly two decades, the President's Commission on Law Enforcement and Administration of Justice, reinforced later by the National Advisory Commission on Criminal Justice Standards, both recommended that police agencies ensure that policies permit qualified women to seek employment, and their usage not be limited to work with juveniles and youths. The Commissions stated clearly that women should serve in patrol and investigative divisions, and that they should assume supervisory and administrative positions as they became qualified.

All of these recommendations were consistent with federal legislation under Title VII of the Civil Rights Act (1972) which prohibits discrimination by employers on the basis of race, creed, color, sex, or national origin. Hence, government agencies, including police departments, are required to prove that unless gender is a "bona fide occupational qualification", they must employ, assign, and advance women on the same basis as men. It is true today that many small departments may employ women in limited numbers, but many that initially employed them in support service roles have now advanced those women to sworn positions. And while it may still hold true that female officers are working in youth bureaus, community relations, vice, and family abuse cases; it is also equally true that there are many hundreds on patrol, many on duty as investigators, and some in supervisory and command ranks.

As more women are assimilated into the patrol units, and gain experience as investigators and supervisors, they will possess the requirements for advancement and gain promotions. Within the past several years, several major cities have announced that they have promoted and assigned a female police commander to be in charge of a district or precinct. Often such a command has several hundred officers working within it.

It might also be worth pointing out here that one distinct advantage to females aspiring to police careers, which has held true throughout the entire history of their employment, has been that equality in pay always did exist. Unlike many other occupations, a women who was employed, completed the academy, was sworn in and assigned to duty, did receive equal pay and benefits as any other entry level police officer. In conjunction with legislative actions, a much greater awareness of career opportunities for women in criminal justice exists now. The implementation of more flexible entrance standards as they relate to height, weight, and strength have continued to result in increased employment of women, and this will continue to occur. Likewise, so will the expansion of duties, assignments, prestige, and authority.

Now that we have discussed in some detail the duties of the patrol officer, let us turn our attention to certain other categories of departmental assignments. Although one may seek or request certain types of assignments, it must always be remembered that the needs of the community, and the priorities of the agency, must come first. There is no real rule of thumb when it comes to specialized duty assignments; some are often long-term by mutual agreement; some are short-term for a variety of reasons; but in nearly all instances, experience is a factor that remains important. Performance, of course, is another.

THE TRAFFIC OFFICER

The officer assigned to the traffic division or traffic bureau spends considerable time directing and controlling the flow of traffic. This function includes, of course, both motor vehicles and pedestrians. In addition to the traffic flow, the officer must be concerned with enforcing parking regulations, although sometimes this is handled by parking enforcement specialists, police cadets, or a specialized unit within the traffic division. Stolen or wanted automobiles are an important part of this unit's total responsibilities, and many such cars are located as a result of relatively minor traffic violations.

The traffic officer frequently is responsible for investigation of abandoned automobiles, as well as their removal. The duties performed are often somewhat similar to personnel of the traffic engineering division, in that reports must be made on the breakdown or inefficiency of traffic control devices.

A very important function of the police traffic specialist relates to the investigation of accidents. Not only must first aid be administered at the scene, but the traffic officer's reports are critical to explaining the causes and recommending any corrections that might be necessary to prevent future crashes. This may include such things as sign dimensions, obstructions to vision, engineering hazards, or driver inattention and bad habits.

The task of issuing traffic citations and making arrests of serious violators belongs to the entire police department, but traffic officers, particularly those on motorcycles, tend to give this greater priority. As in the case of all other police assignments, the traffic enforcement officer spends time testifying in court and frequently becomes involved in civil cases arising out of traffic accidents. Motorists' assistance, escort duty, crowd handling, and rerouting traffic because of a variety of conditions, all place great time demands on those officers concerned with traffic and highway safety. Traffic enforcement that is fair and efficient is very important in permitting all citizens to go about their daily routines.

THE DETECTIVE OR CRIMINAL INVESTIGATOR

Detective work in municipal departments typically begins where the activities of the patrol personnel end. It involves the continuation of investigations, apprehension of any offenders who have been identified, recovery of stolen properties, and again, the all-important tasks of completing official reports and preparing testimony and evidence for court presentation. Detectives do all follow-up interviewing, since the preliminary information-gathering process may have unconnected points in it and may require an analysis which cannot be done easily at the initial scene by the patrol officer.

Another critical task confronting the detective is the actual identification of the offender. This demands that one spend considerable time reviewing physical evidence, clues, interviews, files, background details of the event, and the method of operation, with the ultimate goal of making an identification.

In many ways, the detective is a coordinator of investigations, utilizing the efforts of the patrol officers, laboratory personnel, records clerks, and affected citizens in the quest for accurate information.

Insofar as property is concerned, the detective must obtain a detailed inventory of all stolen items, including serial numbers, labels, markings, and any other distinctive data. The job of recovery requires contact with pawnshops and junk yards, as well as a few persons in the community who make their living through selling stolen articles. These people are popularly referred to as *fences*, and they often operate behind legitimate businesses.

Most detectives are assigned to that position, and departmental policy determines whether it is temporary or permanent. In some departments, the detective status is acquired through examination, in addition to an impressive performance as a patrol officer. Sometimes detectives are rotated back to the patrol unit, and in some departments, detective status is regarded as a promotion, thus becoming a rather permanent assignment, at least until the officer is promoted to a higher rank.

Any successful detective must possess these traits: energy, persistence, courage, initiative, resourcefulness, imagination, accurate memory, good judgment, and powers of observation. Some of these qualities may be gained through training and experience, others are an integral part of one's personality.

As a general rule, detectives specialize in certain kinds of offenses: crimes against *persons*—such as assault, homicide, rape, robbery and those against *property*—notably burglary, theft, and larceny. Detectives may likewise be assigned to juvenile delinquency and youth crimes, or to handling missing persons and school-related offenses. There are also criminal investigative specialists in such technical areas as arson, auto theft, forgery, fraud, narcotics, and the more frequent illegal activities associated with vices (for example, gambling, prostitution, illegal beverages).

Such assignments involve long hours and demand patient and tireless effort, but also carry with them a somewhat higher pay scale, a clothing allowance, and a greater flexibility in terms of working hours and freedom of activity. Also, the detective usually acquires a prestige that is especially attractive to young, aggressive patrol officers.

Team policing, the use of enforcement agents, and other modern approaches to better manpower utilization have attempted to combine the patrol function with that of the criminal investigator or detective. Police departments are performing combined functions within a specific geographic area in this way, by increasing employee responsibility and demanding accountability. Utilizing small groups of personnel and enhancing the opportunity for individual officer decision-making has enabled many departments to obtain better citizen cooperation and minimize the complexities of large organizations and mobile societies. For the educated officer, the challenge is greater, since more personal autonomy can be exerted.

In the recent past, much study and analysis has been conducted on the topic of how criminal investigations are prioritized and managed. Some agencies now utilize the patrol officer to a greater extent in the preliminary investigation, and even during follow-up work when it involves witnesses, records and files originating with the patrol officer, and informants. Future strategies will likely call for more targeted investigations, whereby cases are carefully screened, some are given priorities, resources are more carefully managed, and emphasis is placed upon known, serious, and repeat offenders. A recent federal study provides insight for future policy-making by indicating that most robbery and burglary investigations are solved equally by criminal investigators and patrol officers, that such cases are conducted in a relatively short time span, that leads tend to dissolve after several days, and that the best sources of information are witnesses, informants, police records, and other police officers.

In addition to the specializations mentioned already, the size and demands of the agency will dictate the need for any others.

The following are some of the specialized assignments that complexities of modern police service require.

- Bomb, explosive devices, and arson officers use specialized equipment and training to detect and disarm explosives or suspicious devices and also investigate fires.
- Canine officers are teamed with specially trained dogs to provide special skills in searches, tracking, and crowd control.
- Community relations officers maintain contact and relationships with the police department and the community it serves. They are instrumental in crime prevention efforts and may provide linkage to schools, civic groups, and businesses as a part of their crime reduction and personal safety programs.
- Emergency services or tactical units are specially trained to perform rescues of various kinds. They are called to the scene of life-threatening events and will have special equipment to facilitate their work. Special weapons and tactics teams support patrol units.
- Harbor patrol, helicopter, and short takeoff and landing aircraft are all a part of modern patrol work. Duties of those on such assignments will range from distress and rescue calls, to pursuit of smugglers and observation of ground activities for both safety and surveillance missions.
- Anti-crime or street crime units work in high-crime areas and specialize in overt efforts to fight agressive street crime. They may employ decoy tactics, stakeouts, or high visibility.
- Specialty units may exist for such purposes as dealing with juveniles and youth, sex crimes, vice and narcotics offenses, and any other groups of criminal activities where the need

justifies special attention.
- Additionally, there are assignments to hostage negotiation teams, organized crime sections, intelligence-gathering, and internal affairs.

When one considers further the potential for duty assignments to the training academy, property control, records and identification, laboratory with mobile units, and numerous other less-recognized but highly-demanding areas of responsibility, it is easier to understand why law enforcement is regarded as a diverse and challenging occupation. Police agencies have legal advisors, researchers, data analysts, forensic scientists, computer programmers, and personnel specialists, all of whom could be police officers with long-term career assignments. Some of these could be civilians, too, which will be discussed in a later chapter.

COUNTY UNITS AND SHERIFF'S DEPARTMENTS

Law enforcement career-seekers may want to consider service at the county level of government. Some states have developed county-wide police units which are organized and administered similarly to city departments. In such places, the officer will engage in the same kinds of patrol duties that are found in the city department, except that the county employee may be responsible for a more extensive geographic area. Depending upon the population density, the county officer may find the duties similar in many ways to those of the state police officer. That is, a great variety of services will be performed while covering a broad geographic area, and many of the demands will arise from the smaller communities and unincorporated sections. In several states, notably New York, Kentucky, Texas, Florida, Maryland, and Virginia, certain county police departments are regarded by authorities as some of the nation's finest examples of progress in maintaining law and order.

Often regarded as models of organization and performance, these same county departments have enjoyed very progressive leadership, with chiefs being appointed by the county executive or by a county board of commissioners. County police departments are not to be confused with sheriff's departments, although actual assignments and duties may not be very different. The sheriff is a constitutional officer and is historically and typically an elected official. The sheriff's office is found in most states where county police are not. The sheriff will possess some constitutional powers not generally assigned to the appointed police chief. Depending upon size of the population to be served, the sheriff will employ a force of uniformed deputies and, in many cases, plain clothes investigators. Since sheriffs are responsible for the administration of the county jail, they must also maintain a 24-hour staff in that facility. As a general rule, the sheriff's deputies perform patrol services, investigate offenses, and provide protection in the same manner as do municipal law enforcement officers. Perhaps the most significant difference, other than maintaining the county jail, would be the sheriff's responsibility for serving civil papers and orders of the county courts and transporting prisoners. In recent years, sheriffs' departments have been able to move away from their historical fee system and adopt salary scales that are in many instances competitive with their colleagues in the major cities. More recently, the sheriffs have been able to secure civil service coverage for many of their employees, and while the sheriffs themselves must run for office in a popular election, many have succeeded in securing job protection for their deputies. Like the state police officer, the deputy sheriff can expect to be confronted by a variety of demands. Because such officers usually patrol alone, they must demonstrate resourcefulness and leadership. Deputy sheriffs are actually very much like their municipal counterparts, the significant difference is really in the organization and jurisdiction of the agency itself.

With regard to the differences, deputy sheriffs often serve in the courtroom as bailiffs. They also may act as extradition officers for prisoner escorts, and serve orders or civil papers of the county court, including subpoenas, show-cause orders, property seizures and garnishments. Some deputies are responsible for collecting legal fees assigned by the courts, some have jurisdiction in county parks and game areas, and currently, many have duty protecting court facilities and court officials. Some of the sheriff's departments that employ patrol services have contracted with smaller units of government, perhaps a township, and provide the police services for that community on the basis of the contract. In a circumstance such as this, often considered to be a progressive and productive arrangement, the opportunities for employment may increase, although there may actually be fewer numbers of police agencies in existence there.

One seeking a law enforcement career should certainly not overlook the many townships, boroughs, villages, and modest-sized cities that dominate this nation. While the thrust of this narrative tends to cite illustrations and activities most often identified with the more dense populations, the role of the police does not, in truth, differ that much from a large urban center to a small village or rural county. The events to be responded to and the problems to be solved are often the same; what differs is the frequency with which they occur and the intensity with which the various demands arise. As we note elsewhere in this book, there are anticipated growths in personnel in many of the suburban and mid-sized towns as populations move out from the urban centers. This redistribution of police personnel is underway presently and promises to continue with annexations, contracting, consolidations, and rural America's insistence upon equal services.

Discussions in chapters elsewhere regarding entrance qualifications and procedures, the desirability of higher education, the importance of training, the benefits and advantages of the job, and the potential for advancement and other careers, all will apply at the county level of law enforcement employment. In fact, based upon some recent and rapid population movements to the suburbs, the unincorporated areas, and the smaller communities on the periphery of large cities, one might speculate that county agencies might offer greater potential for employment and expanded career choices.

Law enforcement is making good strides toward greater officer discretion and a sense of personal accomplishment in the work being done by the officer. Whatever managerial techniques are employed, a number of futuristic and progressive departments are encouraging and rewarding greater patrol officer responsibility and initiative. The labels will differ; team policing, master patrol officer, police agent, and various styles of beat coverage will apply; but the ultimate aim is to make a patrol officer's job more enhanced and desirable.

Before concluding the section which discusses local level police service, it might be timely to outline a very ambitious and futuristic plan being undertaken by the District of Columbia Metropolitan Police Department. For nearly two years, the department has been doing some very pro-active planning in order to improve its services. It is worth mentioning here, since it reflects the thinking of the modern police agency, and could well serve as a philosophic goal for those wishing to consider their own employment and future in any police agency. Upon adoption, all officers will receive orientation sessions dealing with the implementation of the concepts and exactly how operational improvements are envisioned to be brought about. In the meantime, departmental task forces have established the plan, which consists of value and belief statements considered essential; these, in turn, provide all personnel with priorities, goals, and directions for the future:

- An improved capability to respond to citizen calls for service, particularly emergency calls requiring the immediate response of an officer.
- An improvement in the delivery of police services through more efficient and productive use of police officers' time while on duty.
- An increased ability to investigate crimes, particularly those crimes that have the greatest potential for being solved.
- An improved ability to identify and apprehend offenders.
- An increased understanding among the police and community regarding each other's problems and priorities through improved communications and citizen invovlement in the police decision-making process.
- Increased job satisfaction and morale among all employees within the department.

Some state law enforcement employees work in prisons and in armories like this one. Photo: State of Illinois, Department of Corrections.

CHAPTER 3

OPPORTUNITIES AT
THE STATE LEVEL

Comparatively new, yet frequently the easiest to recognize of the modern enforcement units, is the one at the state level; whether it be a state police with full criminal enforcement powers or a highway patrol, which may be limited to enforcing the motor vehicle code of a particular state. Because of their twentieth century origin, these departments tend to be free of some of the early municipal police traditions and have generally managed to mature into well-organized, well-trained, and highly respected organizations.

Although several had modest beginnings in 1835 (Massachusetts) and in 1865 (Texas Rangers), most authors refer to 1903 in Pennsylvania as the beginning of a true statewide police agency possessing full enforcement powers. Connecticut in 1903 had a force similar to that of Massachusetts; Arizona in 1901 had a ranger force similar to that in Texas; and New Mexico established mounted police in 1905. Others followed in rapid succession, and today all states except Hawaii have some enforcement unit whose superintendent or director is appointed by the governor and whose jurisdiction is statewide.

Over half of the highway patrols and state police function as one agency within that state's Department of Public Safety. A lesser number operate as separate agencies whose chief administrators report directly to the governor.

The FBI publication, *Crime in the United States*, listed numbers of personnel in these organizations as follows for the year 1983.

FULL-TIME STATE POLICE AND HIGHWAY PATROL EMPLOYEES OCTOBER 1982

		Officers		Civilians	
State	*Total*	*Male*	*Female*	*Male*	*Female*
Alabama	1,175	688	6	185	296
Alaska	825	424	13	103	285
Arizona	1,504	906	28	304	266
Arkansas	628	468	13	63	84
California	7,306	4,917	127	1,025	1,237
Colorado	681	472	9	82	118
Connecticut	1,242	813	21	202	206
Delaware	565	417	8	67	73
Florida	1,830	1,265	39	202	324
Georgia	1,489	801	9	348	331
Idaho	170	137	1	18	14
Illinois	2,054	1,503	42	243	266
Indiana	1,665	1,077	13	288	287
Iowa	776	539	11	105	121
Kansas	565	415	3	81	66
Kentucky	1,612	901	8	396	307
Louisiana	1,176	869	9	100	198
Maine	463	326	3	64	70
Maryland	2,114	1,462	51	216	385
Massachusetts	1,123	924	33	113	53
Michigan	3,072	2,041	53	542	436
Minnesota	615	464	6	101	44
Mississippi	882	552	3	97	230
Missouri	1,613	794	3	558	258
Montana	300				
Nebraska	503	379	4	60	60
Nevada	258	181	2	15	60
New Hampshire	278	215	2	32	29
New Jersey	3,224	1,918	43	760	503
New Mexico	652	378	8	104	162
New York	3,830	3,257	66	153	354
North Carolina	1,419	1,110	3	195	111
North Dakota	123	101	1	2	19
Ohio	1,916	1,128	18	373	397
Oklahoma	1,319	812	12	231	264

| | | Officers | | Civilians | |
State	Total	Male	Female	Male	Female
Oregon	958	816	19	19	541
Pennsylvania	4,799	3,721	56	481	541
Rhode Island	200	163	1	28	8
South Carolina	884	740	9	50	85
South Dakota	184	131		35	18
Tennessee	947	560	4		
Texas	4,706	2,644	37	607	1,418
Utah	444	363	3	20	58
Vermont	382	252	5	50	75
Virginia	1,862	1,304	19	156	383
Washington	1,257	741	8	309	199
West Virginia	823	528	7	85	203
Wisconsin	609	443	7	87	55
Wyoming	205	161		9	35
Totals	66,927	45,221	863	9,364	11,096

From the FBI Uniform Crime Reports, Crime in the United States, 1983.

STATE POLICE AND HIGHWAY PATROL

All state patrol agencies require high school graduation (or the equivalent), and in fact, several now require some amount of college. In Florida for example the Highway Patrol encourages applicants to possess two years of college, but accepts certain work experience or military, in lieu of the higher education. For several years now, both Texas and Washington have given priority to job candidates who possess two years of higher education. With regard to minimum age, there has been a downward trend in the last few years, and approximately one-third of the organizations permit entrance at less than 21 years of age. Another previous requirement experiencing a decline is height, with most of the departments reporting that they no longer have a height minimum. Specific details as to physical requirements can be obtained from the headquarters unit in your state capital. In general, however, there is little difference from those characteristics described for entry into local police service. In other words, to reiterate briefly, candidates may expect qualifying written examinations administered through a civil service, or state merit system. Also, one can expect a rigorous physical exam which is comprehensive and will determine stamina, agility, general suitability to the tasks, and that eyesight and hearing are at acceptable standards. All state agencies with sworn officers to be hired will conduct interviews, and some may require psychological testing or polygraph clearance. Likewise, a very thorough and exhaustive background investigation can be anticipated.

Since both the state police and the highway patrol are quasimilitary units, the rank system begins with private, and, after achieving satisfactory proficiency ratings and service, the trooper can advance to private first class. Then, through written and oral examinations and continuing satisfactory proficiency ratings, the trooper can be promoted from corporal through sergeant and into the ranks of lieutenant, captain, and so on. In almost all departments, the superintendent carries the rank of colonel.

The highway patrol enforces the Motor Vehicle Code and tends to work primarily on state highways, interstate systems, and roads that are in the unincorporated areas of the counties. Gradually, in some states, greater enforcement powers are being delegated to the highway patrol as it becomes clearly evident that the use of the automobile is associated with crime. The state police officer, however, in contrast to the highway patrol, does have full police powers throughout the state, although in practice, the most of the work is in the unincorporated community. In terms of the daily routine, however, the state police officer also spends considerable time enforcing the Motor Vehicle Code on the highways. Either the highway patrol or the state police can legally function in areas where city or town police exist, but, for the most part, they do so only at the request of city officials or upon order from the governor. Such requests and orders are most likely to occur during such emergency situations as natural disasters, civil disorders, or excessive criminal activities that have grown beyond the capability of the local agency.

In general it can certainly be noted that whether state officers are employed by the highway patrol or the state police, their training is lengthy and thorough. It is not unusual for recruits in these departments to undergo four-to-six months' training at recruit academies—during which time they receive intensive firearms and physical training, as well as lectures relating to their many enforcement responsibilities.* The classroom training is always supplemented with field experience so that the new trooper has considerable opportunity to put into practice what he has studied in the academy.**Some of the most rigorous training encountered in a new law enforcement officer's career is that experienced by the trooper. The trooper's day is very similar to that of an army recruit, in that it begins early in the morning with physical training and continues into the evening with study and maintenance of equipment. In addition to classroom hours studying criminal law, traffic ordinances, accident investigation, and community relations, the recruit must practice pursuit driving, first aid, the use of weapons, and completing detailed reports.

With recent increases in assignments of state police officers to urban settings, there has been a major commitment to training in human relations, citizen relationships, and inter-personal skills. In some states, recent attempts to reduce driving under the influence of alcohol and/or drugs have expanded the duties of the trooper far beyond those of routine patrol and accident investigation. State officers may be called upon to assist and support the local police, and this may occur in the form of local traffic control and enforcement or it may include actual back-up actions with full enforcement powers.

Although duty in the state organization may involve some transfers and reassignment to other sections of that state, there is much to be said for the opportunities in either state police or highway patrol units. Troopers nearly always patrol alone and, therefore, must possess versatility and a capacity for taking full

---

*As reported in the *Comparative Data Report* of the International Association of Chiefs of Police, the average number of hours spent by recruits in a training academy is over 600 hours for highway patrols and over 800 hours for state police departments.

**As also reported by the IACP, the average number of hours that recruits spend on the road in supervised field training is 450 hours for highway patrols and 400 hours for the state police.

responsibility in a critical situation. They often perform some distance away from their headquarters and their superiors and must be prepared, through temperament and training, to adapt rapidly to a variety of circumstances. A trooper's day may lead from investigating a fatal traffic crash to the recovery of a stolen automobile or the apprehension of fleeing holdup suspects. In approximately half of the states, the trooper with full police powers may be called upon to handle any crime-related complaint which arises in the unincorporated communities being served. Then, too, at the request of either municipal officials or the governor, the state officer may be called into the incorporated city to reinforce or otherwise aid the local police.

As greater patrol responsibilities have been needed on new expressways and interstate highways, state agencies have been authorized significant increases in personnel strength. There is also a continuing increase of calls to assist local and suburban police, particularly with functions calling for specialized expertise.

CIVILIAN POSITIONS

In addition to uniformed officers, there are numerous civilians employed by the state. The chart on a preceding page shows that almost as many as one-third of the total employees of state police agencies are in fact, civilians. These include technical personnel in state crime laboratories and employees responsible for motor vehicle registration, driver and licensing examinations, and motor vehicle inspection. A young person interested in such employment should contact the headquarters unit in the state capital for detailed information and specific requirements.

Consider the magnitude of employment required to operate the computers and maintain the legal requirements associated with auto registrations, other vehicles, drivers and commercially licensed operators, and violations that must be recorded. Also, all injury and some property-damage crashes must be recorded and analyzed. Writers, photographers, clerical halp, mathematicians, and technicians of various kinds are needed in many different departments.

OTHER REGULATORY UNITS

Duty at the state level is by no means restricted to the state police or the highway patrol. A number of regulatory, licensing, and protective functions exist which also require competent personnel. Examples of these many agencies are included in a list from the state of California.

This listing was chosen because it is perhaps the most inclusive insofar as state responsibility for licensing and regulation goes. It can be assumed that all states have these various functions performed in some manner, but all may not be accomplished through specific departments and agencies. A young person interested in pursuing a career that includes significant enforcement responsibilities but has as its main purpose something other than traditional policing would be well advised to consider some of these employment opportunities. For instance, someone particularly interested in outdoor activities and nature might consider a career in one of a number of state regulatory agencies which have as their primary purpose the protection of wildlife or the preservation of our natural surroundings. Certain state agencies exercise limited policing functions in such widely diversified fields as communications, public health, transportation, and welfare. Again, an individual might select a career which would permit him to satisfy his interest in the enforcement task, yet pursue another goal which is not necessarily limited to policing. An example of this might be conducting investigations for the state fire marshal's office or working at the many inspections performed by state agents—from food and drugs to horse racing and industrial safety.

GOVERNMENTAL UNITS POSSESSING POLICE POWER IN THE STATE OF CALIFORNIA

Department of Agriculture

Division of Dairy Industry
  Bureau of Milk Stabilization
Division of Compliance
  Bureau of Livestock Identification
  Bureau of Market Enforcement
  Bureau of Weights and Measures
Division of Plant Industry
  Bureau of Plant Quarantine
  Bureau of Plant Pathology
Division of Animal Industry
  Bureau of Animal Health
  Bureau of Dairy Service
  Bureau of Meat Inspection
  Bureau of Poultry Inspection

Department of Alcoholic Beverage Control

Youth and Adult Corrections Agency
Department of Corrections
Adult Authority
Board of Trustees of the
California Institution for
Women
Adult Parole Division
Department of Youth Authority

California Disaster Office
Law Enforcement Division

Department of California Highway Patrol

Department of Education
Division of Departmental
Administration
California Program for Peace
Officers' Training

Department of Employment
Division of Public Employment
Offices and Benefit Payments

Department of Finance
Building and Grounds Division
California State Police

Department of Industrial Relations
Division of Housing
Division of Industrial Welfare
Industrial Welfare Commission
Division of Industrial Safety
Division of Labor Law Enforcement
Fair Employment Practice
Commission

Department of Insurance
Compliance and Legal Division
Policy Complaints Bureau

Department of Investments
Division of Corporations
Division of Real Estate
Division of Savings and Loan

Department of Justice
Division of Criminal Law and
Enforcement
Bureau of Criminal Identification
and Investigation
Bureau of Narcotic Enforcement

Department of Mental Hygiene

Department of Motor Vehicles
Division of Registration
Division of Drivers' Licenses
Division of Field Office Operation

Department of Professional and Vocational Standards
Division of Investigation
Board of Accountancy
Board of Architectural Examiners
Athletic Commission
Board of Barber Examiners
Cemetery Board
Board of Chiropractic Examiners
Board of Registration for Civil
and Professional Engineers
Contractors' State License Board
Board of Cosmetology
Board of Dental Examiners
Bureau of Private Investigators
and Adjusters
Board of Dry Cleaners
Board of Funeral Directors and
Embalmers
Board of Furniture and Bedding
Inspection
Board of Guide Dogs for the
Blind
Board of Medical Examiners
Board of Nursing Education and
Nurse Registration
Board of Optometry
Board of Pharmacy
Board of Social Work Examiners
Structural Pest Control Board
Board of Examiners in Veterinary
Medicine
Yacht and Ship Brokers'
Commission
Board of Vocational Nurse
Examiners
Collection Agency Licensing
Bureau
Board of Landscape Architects
The Certified Shorthand
Reporters' Board

Department of Public Health
Bureau of Communicable Diseases
Bureau of Sanitary Engineering
Bureau of Hospitals
Bureau of Foods and Drugs
Inspection
Division of Laboratories

Resources Agency
Department of Parks and Recreation
Division of Beaches and Parks
Department of Conservation
Division of Forestry
Division of Mines and Geology
Division of Oil and Gas
Department of Fish and Game

Wildlife Protection Branch

San Francisco Port Authority
Harbor Police

Department of Social Work

State Fire Marshal

Office of Consumer Counsel

Board of Equalization
Department of Business Taxes

State Board of Osteopathic Examiners

California Horse Racing Board
Bureau of Investigations
License Bureau

Of course, it's entirely possible that not all of the above agencies operate in your state; however, it is quite probable that the functions are performed by someone. A wise course of action would be to visit or write the Office of the Governor, or a State Administrator, such as the Secretary of State or the office of your local State Senator or Representative.

Thus, employment options at the state level are not at all limited; whether the assignment be parks, recreational areas, historical monuments, pollution violations, health hazards, communicable diseases, fire prevention, wildlife protection, dairy and livestock regulation, insurance fraud, industrial safety or literally hundreds of other critical areas, one thing remains clear: there is job diversity.

The following list will assist the job aspirant in making direct contact with State Police and Highway Patrol Headquarters:

Department of Public Safety
Coliseum Boulevard
Montgomery, Alabama 36109

State Troopers Division
Department of Public Safety
State Office Building
Juneau, Alaska 99801

Arizona Highway Patrol
Department of Public Safety
2010 West Encanto Boulevard
Phoenix, Arizona 85009

Police Services Division
Department of Public Safety
3701 West Roosevelt
Little Rock, Arkansas 72204

California Highway Patrol
2611 26th Street
Sacramento, California 95814

California State Police
915 Capitol Mall
Office Building #1
Sacramento, California 95814

Colorado State Patrol
4201 East Ark Avenue
Denver, Colorado 80222

Connecticut State Police
100 Washington Street
Hartford, Connecticut 06106

State Police Division
P.O. Box 151
Dover, Delaware 19901

Florida Highway Patrol
Neil Kirkman Building
Tallahassee, Florida 32304

Georgia State Police
Department of Public Safety
959 East Confederate
    Avenue, S.E.
Atlanta, Georgia 30301

Department of the
    Attorney General
State Capitol Building
Honolulu, Hawaii 96813

State Police
Department of Law Enforcement
3211 State Street
Boise, Idaho 83703

State Highway Police
Armory Building
Springfield, Illinois 62706

Indiana State Police
100 North Senate Avenue
Indianapolis, Indiana 46204

State Capitol Police
State Capitol Building
Des Moines, Iowa 50309

State Highway Patrol
1st Floor Office Building
Topeka, Kansas 66612

Division of State Police
Department of Public Safety
State Office Building
Frankfort, Kentucky 40601

State Police Division
Department of Public Safety
P.O. Box 1791
Baton Rouge, Louisiana 70821

Maine State Police
36 Hospital Street
Augusta, Maine 04330

Maryland State Police
1201 Reistertown Road
Pikesville, Maryland 21208

Massachusetts State Police
1010 Commonwealth Avenue
Boston, Massachusetts 02215

Michigan State Police
714 South Harrison Road
East Lansing, Michigan 48823

Minnesota Highway Patrol
State Highway Building
St. Paul, Minnesota 55101

Mississippi Highway Patrol
Public Safety Department
P.O. Box 958
Jackson, Mississippi 39205

State Highway Patrol
1710 Elm Street
Jefferson City, Missouri 65101

Montana Highway Patrol
Hustad Center
Helena, Montana 59601

State Patrol
14th and Burnham
Lincoln, Nebraska 68509

Nevada State Highway Patrol
555 Wrightsway
Carson City, Nevada 89701

State Police Division
New Hampshire Department of
Safety
85 Loudon Road
Concord, New Hampshire 03301

State Police Division
Route 29
West Trenton, New Jersey 08628

New Mexico State Police
P.O. Box 1628
Santa Fe, New Mexico 87501

Division of State Police
State Campus, Building 22
Albany, New York 12226

Highway Patrol
Department of Motor Vehicles
New Bern Avenue
Raleigh, North Carolina 27602

North Dakota Highway Patrol
State Capitol
Bismarck, North Dakota 58501

State Highway Patrol
660 East Main Street
Columbus, Ohio 43205

Highway Patrol
Department of Public Safety
Box 11415
Oklahoma City, Oklahoma 73111

Department of State Police
Public Service Building
Salem, Oregon 97301

Pennsylvania State Police
617 Highway Safety Building
Harrisburg, Pennsylvania 17120

Rhode Island State Police
P.O. Box 185
North Scituate,
    Rhode Island 02857

Highway Patrol
State Highway Department
1100 Senate Street
Columbia, South Carolina 29201

South Dakota Highway Patrol
Highway Office Building
Pierre, South Dakota 57501

Highway Patrol Division
Department of Safety
Cordell Hull Building
Nashville, Tennessee 37219

Texas Rangers
Department of Public Safety
Box 4087 North Austin Station
Austin, Texas 78751

Highway Patrol
Department of Public Safety
State Office Building
Salt Lake City, Utah 84101

Vermont State Police
Public Safety Department
Bailey Avenue Extension
Montpelier, Vermont 05602

Department of State Police
P.O. Box 1299
Richmond, Virginia 23210

Washington State Patrol
Headquarters General
    Administration Building
Olympia, Washington 98501

West Virginia State Police
Capitol Building
Charleston, West Virginia 25305

State Patrol
4845 East Washington
Madison, Wisconsin 53700

Highway Patrol
Wyoming Highway Department
P.O. Box 1708
Cheyenne, Wyoming 82001

National Park rangers are in frequent communication with one another, monitoring activities throughout the park. Photo: United States Department of the Interior, National Park Service.

CHAPTER 4

MILITARY AND FEDERAL SERVICES

Opportunities for young persons exist in the military services and it is not at all unusual to find civilian police personnel who attribute their initial career interest in law enforcement to experience gained while serving in the military police, air police, shore patrol, or in some of the military investigative units such as the Criminal Investigation Command or the Naval Investigative Service.

The Uniform Code of Military Justice is enforced by the military police and no one should overlook the opportunity to gain this experience. There are ample opportunities for specialized schools, patrol and investigative work, promotion through the military ranks, world-wide assignments, and entrance can be accomplished well ahead of the age of twenty-one years.

The military affords a young person the opportunity to learn much about law enforcement, gain valuable training, and can be instrumental in helping one's decision about a career in the field. Some use the military experience as their departure point into civilian policing; others remain for an entire career with the military. The Military Police are found wherever troops are stationed and primarily their duties resemble those of local level law officers, the difference being that they operate on military bases, patrol areas where the military are located, and are generally limited in their jurisdictional activities to military personnel, or persons who are involved in illegal activities aimed toward military personnel.

Since one may join the armed services well ahead of the age when many local agencies or federal organizations will hire, there are some real advantages in terms of experience and training for considering the military. Wise police administrators, and government bureau chiefs welcome candidates who possess military experience, because such applicants are known to already have attained a sense of maturity and responsibility.

FEDERAL AGENCIES

All federal agencies have specific violation categories in which their jurisdiction lies, and the listing in Chapter 8, which was largely taken from the *United States Government Organization Manual*, lists the official responsibilities and duties for each organization. Because of the many diverse opportunities available throughout the federal government, it would be advisable to obtain detailed qualifications directly from the unit in which one is interested. We have, therefore, included addresses in order to assist interested persons in obtaining career brochures. Many federal agencies exert considerable effort on recruitment and respond well to job inquiries.

Most, but not all, federal agencies require a bachelor's degree, and all expect it of those who aspire to promotion. They do not, however, always require it for entrance. Some federal agencies are more investigative-than enforcement-oriented and, therefore, may demand a variety of skills, such as legal training or tax knowledge. The Drug Enforcement Administration needs a variety of persons trained in pharmacy, while the Border Patrol requires persons who speak Spanish fluently. Also, many federal officers find that they spend a great deal of time on a particular case or series of cases. Customs agents might spend a great deal of time investigating a smuggling incident; the Internal Revenue Service agent with accounting skills often devotes long hours to verifying failures to pay proper taxes; the Secret Service cannot relax for one moment its watchful protection of the President and Vice President; and the FBI agent might require many months to solve a violation involving our national security.

Because their numbers are comparatively small and their salaries and prestige relatively great, federal agents possess high personal qualifications and must survive intensive background investigations. Of the large numbers of applicants for federal work, only the best qualified are selected. Attributes of all federal officers include patience and determination. They must be capable of working long hours, willing to travel on a moment's notice, and in some cases, operate virtually alone for prolonged periods. Travel outside of the United States is required in certain departments, and unlike local police officers, the federal agent may devote lengthy periods of time to only a few specialized investigations and make few arrests. The federal role also entails detailed reports and court appearances. Federal agents must be articulate, able to deal with all levels of society, and must always perform as symbolic representatives of American justice. A 20-year retirement in most federal agencies, with pension dependent upon salary attained, makes early departure from government service possible. Many take advantage of this retirement program, thereby creating vacancies in federal units on a continuing basis. In recent years, increasing requests for more federal assistance have resulted in enlargements for most of these organizations. As population expands, additional demands for aid arise, and criminal mobility continues, it can be safely predicted that the United States government will require large numbers of well-qualified and dedicated young persons to fill these important law enforcement positions.

Specific duties of each federal agency appear in the *Organization Manual*, and from it one may learn the official description of a particular agency's work. Educational requirements for most federal agencies include a bachelor's degree. You will find a discussion of salary, taken from the current GS scale, later in the text. Most law enforcement jobs are at the GS 7, 8, or 9 entrance level.

There is no particular "magic" to entering federal service. The applicant *must* apply directly to the agency (see addresses later in chapter). Upon submission of the application, successful completion of the Federal Service Entrance Examiniation is required. Certain aencies may require tests for memory and retention in addition to the general federal entrance exam. All agencies will require the submission of medical data and will make character and background investigations and reference checks. All federal enforcement agencies have their own basic training programs, which vary in length up to 6 months. These are designed to equip the new agent with skills needed in the field. A great deal of the course content relates to federal statues and investigative procedures.

One of the important features of federal enforcement is the continuing in-service training which officers and agents receive. This is, of course, very desirable throughout all law enforcement, but is practiced most regularly and effectively at the federal level. Since most agencies have divided the country into field service offices, it is essential that the prospective federal agent recognize that travel is a necessary part of his job. On the other hand, an attraction to federal service is the 20-year retirement plan, with a lifelong pension amounting to a percentage of one's highest salary. This plan enables one to complete a federal career while he is still relatively young, then pursue different employment. It might be noted that a number of college criminal justice professors and local police chiefs are retired from the federal service.

TYPICAL ASSIGNMENTS*

Let us look at each of the major federal investigative departments and review the particular assignments one could expect to have as a member of these organizations. By way of explanation, it is our intention to cite only those duties which can be regarded as truly enforcement-oriented, and not to include in this narrative any references to the many other jobs in those departments that have to do with planning, communications, training, maintenance, records, data, and information distribution.

The positions described and referenced throughout this chapter all require an ability to recognize and develop evidence for presentation to U.S. Attorneys, to meet and confer with persons engaged

*Criminal Justice Careers Guidebook, U.S. Dept of Labor, Washington DC 20213 (1982)

in many kinds of activities, to testify effectively in a court of law, to prepare detailed written reports, to operate a motor vehicle, to be proficient in the use of firearms and self-defense, and to exercise continual good judgment, resourcefulness, and initiative.

The *U.S. Postal Service*, formerly the Post Office Department, was established independently in 1970. *Postal inspectors* conduct criminal investigations related to losses and thefts of the mail or property owned by the post office. In addition, investigators and security force personnel are charged with protecting postal buildings and installations.

There are some 85 postal-related laws which are encompassed within such duties as mail box thefts, robberies of postal authorities, embezzlements, frauds using the mails, and post office burglaries. There are also attempts to sell items by mail, obtain funds through fraudulent schemes, and other such acts which may be violations of postal laws. If anyone uses the mail system illegally, as in transporting firearms, narcotics, obscene materials, or incendiary devices, they are likewise the subject of investigation and prosecution by postal inspectors. As is the case with many other Federal agents, a very modern crime laboratory is available to support complex investigations.

Several major agencies, employing a total of almost 15,000 criminal investigators, operate within the United States Department of Justice. Probably best known is the *Federal Bureau of Investigation*, and *agents* of this unit are responsible for the enforcement of a rather extensive variety of statues. The FBI agent may be assigned to matters concerning national security, rights' violations, offenses involving interstate transportation, and the security of both personnel employed by the federal government and property owned by the government. Also within the jurisdiction of the FBI are numerous federal acts that pertain to specific offenses, such as bank robbery, kidnapping, and extortion.

Some 200 different types of cases fall within the jurisdiction of the FBI. Certain offenses can be very complicated and involve "white-collar" crimes as in the case of embezzlements in banks, or organized crime activities. From espionage to bankruptcy, the FBI agent examines and evaluates many different types of information and evidence before presenting it to the Department of Justice for prosecution. Most agents are assigned to one of the 59 divisional offices, although some work at the headquarters in Washington and others in resident agencies around the country.

The FBI operates one of the most outstanding crime laboratories in the world, and all types of examinations may be conducted to assist the agents in the field, or to support investigations by local authorities.

The *Immigration and Naturalization Service*, another part of the Department of Justice, administers our nation's immigration and naturalization laws and is responsible for investigations concerning aliens. Its uniformed agents, referred to as the *Border Patrol*, are on continuous duty guarding all U.S. points of entry.

The Border Patrol is highly mobile, uniformed, and its primary areas of work entail detecting and preventing illegal entry into the United States. Agents patrol designated areas and also inspect commercial carriers, terminals and traffice check points to detect aliens and others who attempt to enter the country without proper clearance. It is the Border Patrol which has responsibility for deportation actions also.

INS investigators, unlike the uniformed Border Patrol, review applications for visas, determine whether aliens may enter or remain in the country, and gather all pertinent information relative to the administrative hearings and criminal prosecution of immigration law violations.

U.S. Marshals execute and enforce commands and orders of federal courts, process federal prisoners, seize property under court order, and protect federal judges, witnesses, and juries. The Marshals Service is the oldest of all Federal law enforcement agencies was established during the period of the "Old West." Their major duties have remained similar to the original ones which were to attend to the Federal Courts and execute the orders of the United States Government. Deputy U.S. Marshals are assigned special duties as the needs arise, but basically they still serve both civil and criminal processes of the courts, serve federal warrants, move and protect federal prisoners, witnesses, jurors, and other trial participants, seize property under federal court orders, and handle the collection of federal funds and protect facilities. The role of the Deputy Marshal has always been vital in the area of civil disturbances, and in 1971 a Special Operations Group was established to provide immediate Federal response to civil situations. In recent years, also, the deputy marshals have provided protection for witnesses under the Organized Crime Acts, for missiles being transported, for airline passengers in conjunction with aircraft hijacking, and many other special assignments. There are approximately 2000 such persons with U.S. Marshal sworn authority.

The Drug Enforcement Administration, previously called the Bureau of Narcotics and Dangerous Drugs, is primarily responsible for enforcing laws concerning all narcotic drugs. It also has jurisidiction over the registration provisions of federal drug laws, the combatting or illicit narcotics traffic, and the control of illegal distribution of dangerous drugs. This unit has critical responsibility for determining the quantities of narcotics permissible in the country for medical purposes. In recent years, a sizeable increase in positions has occurred within this federal agency. Some 2,000 DEA agents operate in the U.S. and over forty foreign countries.

It is DEA's goal to identify and eliminate any illegal sources of drug supply and distribution. Many of these sources are overseas, thus necessitating a variety of strategies involving foreign countries. Drug suppression and interdicting of drug trafficking have become very high priorities with the federal government in recent years, and it is the DEA which has the primary role in assisting local agencies.

The largest number of federal criminal investigators (20,000) is employed within the agencies operating under the *U.S. Department of the Treasury*. One of these agencies is the *Customs Service*, which is concerned with regulating the importation of goods into the country. The Customs Service is especially concerned with smuggling activities which may occur in our ports of entry. This Bureau also has many responsibilities pertaining to goods being shipped into or from this country. *Customs agents* might find their daily duties varying from examining an incoming traveler's luggage to registering the weight of an incoming vessel. Customs Service enforces some 400 laws and regulations for the federal government; in a sense this organization insures that revenue is paid for incoming goods while restricting the flow of prohibited goods from entering or leaving the country. Their priorities include not only the protection of the revenue system, but the health and safety of our citizens. There are several different job levels within the Customs Service and include Special Agents, Customs Officers, Import Specialists, and Customs Inspectors. Quite naturally, these personnel work vary closely with DEA, INS and FBI in dealing with baggage, merchandise, cargo, and other potential locations of tax abuse.

Also under the Treasury Department is the *Internal Revenue Service*. In general, IRS *agents'* assignments encompass the U.S. tax revenue system. Agents of this organization, many of whom are professional accountants, perform a variety of duties, including examination of taxpayers' records to determine tax liabilities, as well as investigation of cases involving tax fraud or evasion of tax payments (such as those pertaining to business or gambling).

Within the Treasury Department are special investigators of the *Alcohol, Tobacco, and Firearms Bureau*. Their duties relate to the enforcement of federal laws governing the manufacture, sale, distribution, and possession of firearms and explosives, alcohol, and tobacco products. Agents of this division are assigned to regulate and maintain records on the legal taxable production of alcoholic beverages and have authority to apprehend those engaged in illegal activities relating to alcholic beverages. ATF agents direct much of their effort against terrorist groups, organized crime, and those involved in bombing incidents. Perhaps best known for their work in illicit distillery investigations, the ATF also is empowered to seize and destroy illegal production and distribution networks, and to reduce the smuggling of contraband cigarettes and other untaxed tobacco products.

The *Secret Service* has a twofold responsibility: that of protecting the President and Vice President of the United States, along with the members of their families, and the protection of the coins and securities of the government through enforcement of the laws pertaining to counterfeiting. With over 2,000 agents, the Secret Service also protects the White House, the Treasury Building, and its Foreign Missions Branch and is charged with the protection of foreign embassies.

Prior to 1978, the Secret Service, which dates back to 1922, operated the White House Police Force; this later became the Executive Protection Service and now is known as the Uniformed Division. Under their officers continuous protection are all of the Executive Mansion and its grounds; buildings in which White House offices are located; foreign diplomatic missions and residences in certain cases; and now the official residence of the Vice President as well.

For the most part the counterfeiting investigations conducted by the U.S. Secret Service Special Agent involve stolen checks, bonds, and securities. The forgery of any currency or the forging of signatures in order to cash any governmental obligation such as a check, is the exclusive jurisdiction of this agency and they enjoy an extremely high rate of success in prosecutions.

Federal Protective Officers are under the control of the *General Services Administration*; they are uniformed and authorized the protect property and life within areas under the control of the GSA. In other words, federally owned and operated buildings, adjacent ground and parking areas, vulnerable entry points, and the like are all monitored or secured in some fashion so that law and order are maintained on government property.

The U.S. Office of Personnel Management, formerly known as the U.S. Civil Service Commission, maintains a Register or Listing of qualified candidates for many of the positions which have been described in this section. It is imperative that contact be made with that office in order to establish the basic qualifications necessary for any particular position and to obtain the proper application forms and other related materials. One should plan well ahead in pursuing federal jobs because the turnover is often low, the salary and benefits are significant, and there may well be a time lag between first inquiry and being placed officially on the qualified list and then being hired.

Within the federal government, there are many other units with enforcement and supervisory responsibilities, such as the Federal Aviation Administration, Occupational Safety and Health Administration, Mining Enforcement and Safety Administration,

Many forest rangers do most of their work outdoors. Photo: United States Department of the Interior, National Park Service.

Public Health Service, Bureau of Sport Fisheries and Wildlife, and Food and Drug Administration. For example, there are over 7,000 *federal food inspectors*, as well as 2,600 *investigators* employed to check on compliance with civil rights statues. Even less known to the general public, but still offering attractive career opportunities, are such federal positions as the nearly 600 *U.S. Civil Service Commission investigators*, and 150 *Consumer Product Safety Commission investigators*. In addition, the person who enjoys farm and rural life should not overlook the fact that over 8,400 *investigators* work for the *Agriculture Department*. For those interested in game, wildlife, and outdoor recreation, the *Department of the Interior* employs nearly 2,200 *investigators* for its parks and wildlife refuges. Also not to be overlooked is the *General Services Administration*, which employs nearly 3,500 persons to conduct criminal and civil investigations that relate to collusion, bribery, conflicts of interest, thefts from government jurisdictions, and offenses specified within the acts protecting government personnel and procedures.

In addition to the large and well-known federal enforcement organizations, there are a considerable number of *independent agencies* whose responsibilities involve enforcement of a highly specialized and technical nature. Some of these include the Federal Communications Commission, Federal Maritime Commission, Federal Power Commission, Nuclear Regulatory Commission, Federal Trade Commission, Federal Emergency Management Agency, National Aeronautics & Space Administration, and Interstate Commerce Commission.

Beyond criminal investigative positions in the federal government, there are numerous *intelligence specialists* whose primary duties relate to background clearances and security personnel matters. These include persons employed by the Central Intelligence Agency, National Security Agency, Defense Intelligence Agency, and special agents of the Department of State.

Interested young people are urged to contact these federal agencies directly, because all of them have specific career information available.

The listing provided in Chapter 8 describes the legal respon-

Department of Defense

Dept. of the Army
Pentagon Headquarters
Washington, DC 20310

Dept. of the Air Force
Pentagon Headquarters
Washington, DC 20330

Dept. of the Navy
Pentagon Headquarters
Washington, DC 20350

Department of Health and Human Services

Public Health Service
5600 Fishers Lane
Rockville, MD 20852

Food and Drug Admin.
5600 Fishers Lane
Rockville, MD 20852

Department of the Interior

Bureau of Indian Affairs
1951 Constitution Avenue N.W.
Washington DC 20245

National Park Service
Interior Department Bldg
Washington DC 20240

Fish and Wildlife Service
1612 K Street, N.W.
Washington DC 20240

Department of Justice

Federal Bureau of Investigation
Ninth Street & Pennsylvania
Avenue, N.W.
Washington DC 20537

Federal Bureau of Prisons
320 First Street N.W.
Washington DC 20534

Drug Enforcement Administration
1405 Eye Street N.W.
Washington DC 20537

Immigration & Naturalization Service
425 Eye Street N.W.
Washington DC 20536

U.S. Marshals Service
One Tysons Corner Center
McLean, VA 22102

Department of State

Recruitment & Employment Division
Washington DC 20520

Department of Agriculture

Office of Inspector General
Washington DC 20250

Department of Labor

200 Constitution Avenue, N.W.
Washington DC 20210

U.S. Department of Commerce

Office of the Inspector General
Washington DC 20005

Department of the Treasury

Bureau of Alcohol, Tobacco, &
   Firearms
1111 Constitution Avenue N.W.
Washington DC 20226

U.S. Customs Service
1301 Constitution Avenue N.W.
Washington DC 20229

Internal Revenue Service
1111 Constitution Avenue, N.W.
Washington DC 20224

U.S. Secret Service
1800 G Street, N.W.
Washington DC 20223

Department of Transportation

U.S. Coast Guard
400 Seventh Street S.W.
Washington DC 20590

General Services Administration

General Services Bldg
Office of Personnel
18th & F Streets N.W.
Washington DC 20405

U.S. Postal Service
475 L'Enfant Plaza
Inspection Services Office
Washington DC 20260

United States Congress
Capitol Police
U.S. Capitol Bldg
Washington DC 20510

Additional Agencies

Agency of International Development
Washington DC 20523

Environmental Protection Agency
401 "M" Street, S.W.
Washington DC 20460

For additional assistance and information: Office of Personnel Management, 1900 E. Street, Washington DC 20415.

CHAPTER 5

SALARIES AND
EMPLOYMENT CONDITIONS

The salary progress that law enforcement has achieved in very recent years is certainly related to several factors; the state standardization of training; the awarding of certification; educational progress toward individual professional stature; and a general increase in public support and community recognition of the duties of police officers. Starting and maximum salaries are both quite competitive with the salaries offered by other employers who seek personnel of the same age, educational level and experience.

The average pay for police officers has increased some 50% in the last decade, and large numbers of police patrol officers now work in cities where the maximum salary is over $20,000. In the late 1970's, average starting salaries were slightly above $12,000. By the early 1980's, those same city averages showed an increase up to nearly $15,000.

Let us look at some starting or entrance level salaries as they are reported by selected cities in 1983. San Jose, California advertises for starting patrol officers at $25,893 and increasing within 4 years up to $31,473. The city of Pasadena, California similarly starts one at $25,764 and will offer increases over three years up to $29,232. Historically, California has led the nation in police salaries. In 1979, San Diego was slightly higher than what the national city average has attained by 1983. It should also be noted that cities such as San Diego require that police candidates have significant educational achievements, up to and including two year degrees. In

Bellevue, Washington, another city requiring two years of education above high school, the starting salary for a patrol officer offered is $22,2$1 and can reach $28,464.

The Metro-Dade (Florida) County Police Department starts an officer at $20,200 while still in the Academy, and the top of scale is $25,500. Considering that one can apply, be employed, and attend the Academy at age 19, this is a significant career beginning. In Dallas, Texas, the police recruit can start at a salary of $21,060 and must have over one year of college. With a degree, Dallas starts an officer at $22,260.

The city of Orlando Florida is probably closer to the typical or average situation in terms of police earnings. An officer begins at $15,221 and progresses to a top patrol officer figure of $19,658. In Alexandria, Virginia, a Washington D.C. suburb, the starting police salary is $18,015 and one can reach $25,290 after a number of years of service. A Bachelor's degree in this instance will add another $1000 annually. On the other side of the country, in Seattle, Washington, an officer starts with a salary of $21,672 and may reach to $26,880 after only four years service.

As we have demonstrated, salaries will vary; sometimes because of the type of agency and its size; sometimes because of geographic differences which reflect themselves in industrial competition; sometimes due to historical reasons and how public employment has fared generally in that region over the course of time.

Continuing with some other important salary illustrations; Detroit, Michigan has a starting police salary of $21,184 and one can go up to $26,296 without a promotion. In Pennsylvania, the Philadelphia police department has a beginning salary of $19,936 and reaches $22,671 after several steps.

To again illustrate the variations within a rather close geographical area, consider that the capital city of Harrisburg Starts officers at $17,339 and nearby Northern York Regional Police begins officers at $15,440; however by the second year, Harrisburg is at $18,541 and the York Regional salaries will be $22,300. It is good advice to make careful comparisons that reach beyond a basic entrance level figure. How many pay steps are there before reaching the top of the officer scale? What financial reward does promotion bring, and is it significantly higher than the officer rank?

It has been observed often that law enforcement enjoys higher salaries than those associated with some other public service careers and other categories of public employment. These include social workers, nurses, public school teachers, and other critical roles in which education and training have always been required. Furthermore, the evidence continues to mount that policing is a career field on the move; income levels are rising, many officers receive overtime for extra duty, special hazard pay is often available for certain assignments, and many states now award incentive pay for educationsl and training attainments.

Some estimates now are that as many as half of all cities offer increases in salary for education and/or training. A decade ago, the figure was only 37% reporting such programs for incentive. A typical salary incentive pay plan may add an additional $50 per month to the salary for an Associate degree and $100 per month for the Bachelor's degree.

Present students may be well advised to seek out those agencies where incentive pay is made available for higher education; not merely for the additional salary it offers one, but even more importantly, it suggests a commitment to professional stature and top quality that is most important in seeking one's career affiliation. A good rule of thumb, for career guidance, is to look at the basic salary for academy study and immediately upon entrance, the range that exists for entry positions, and what the top level command jobs pay.

Quite obviously, salary variations are important to anyone seeking a career, and it is always advisable to obtain the latest salary figures from the specific department of interest. This information is not difficult to obtain and will usually be quoted in any job vacancy notice, even in local newspapers and ads. With contract negotiations occuring in many jurisdictions, and with the general fiscal priorities which police protection enjoys, a salary quoted in print may be somewhat out of date by the time the applicant is sworn into the position.

All recruiting notices and announcements should outline the details of salary and fringe benefits, as well as required work week, paid holidays, policy for leaves and sick benefits, life insurance, and so forth. But it must be emphasized that because all of these matters are constantly improving, no figures or amounts should be regarded as definitive unless they are from the agency's own official notice. And again, extra pay may be available for hazardous duty with motorcycles, helicopters, patrol boats, or as a dog handler, to say nothing of overtime, about which one has little choice.

It may also be that officers will be paid additional percentages for midnight shift duty or for teaching in the Academy during off-duty hours. Of course, promotion to higher rank brings additional income. In most jurisdictions, assignment to the detective or investigative unit adds additional salary also.

It would be difficult, indeed, in a national publication to attempt to discuss salaries above those at the entry level. It can be assumed that moving up the rank structure brings with it monetary increases, and these are in addition to normal pay raises that typically occur as a result of longevity (time in the organization). One method of gaining insight into the career potential for remuneration is to look at what the top jobs pay. Again, they demonstrate a wide variation. Some sheriffs who serve as constitutional officers, some state police superintendents who serve as members of the Governor's cabinet, and some large city chiefs of police earn in the range of $60,000. To cite a few examples beyond that, consider that the Chief of Police in Detroit was salaried in late 1983 at a figure of $57,000. In our nation's capital, Washington D.C., the chief's salary is about $65,000.

This represents a significant increase at that level of the organization when one remembers that the previous edition of this book, only some four years ago, quoted chiefs in the largest cities as earning around $35,000, and several top state administrators as being in the $40,000 category. One of these, the Pennsylvania State Police Commissioner, has now reached a salary level of over $51,000.

Clearly, not all careerists can expect to achieve the position of chief of police in their particular locale, and salaries such as Commissioner in New York City or Chief in Los Angeles may not really be typical anywhere else. But there are, in fact, many high level positions that do enjoy comparatively high salaries. The titles of *deputy chief, assistant chief, deputy commissioner,* along with *lieutenant colonels* and *majors,* all attain salaries only slightly less than that of the top administrator, and these are realistic goals for the serious career minded professional.

One should remember that while there may be only one chief, sheriff, or director, there may be a team supporting policy decisions made up of a half-dozen top command personnel, and all of these officials will most likely have been the products of that organization and will be paid at salaries well within reach of the chief's. Again, to use our illustration of the Metro Dade (FL) Police Department, the current range for a Division Chief, of which there are several, is $45,000 up to $65,000.

FRINGE BENEFITS

In addition to competitive salaries, enforcement agencies traditionally have offered many fringe benefits that are either comparable to or exceed those of private industry. For many years, law enforcement has advertised and prided itself on the retirement system it made available to officers. Likewise, sick and injury leave provisions have been attractive. Generally speaking, after twenty years of service, an officer can retire with a specific percentage of one's highest salary. Most likely, this can be done at age 55. Should the employee remain with the agency for 25 or more years, the percentage of salary paid for retirement increases accordingly. If one were to take this retirement at age 55 in law enforcement, consider that someone else having worked in business or industry would have another 10 years to work before the usual retirement age of 65.

Group health and life insurance programs are universal in law enforcement work. Vacation, Holiday, and other leave arrangements are a routine part of any jurisdiction's policies and will not vary greatly among communities. Of course, disability insurance exists in the event an officer is injured in the line of duty.

Local level law enforcement provides relatively good job security, most likely through a form of civil service or local merit system.

Then too, many more communities now have unions or police employee associations to afford further job protection.

Again, as with salaries and upward mobility, any job applicant should ask questions about fully paid hospitatlization insurance, the inclusion of dental and vision plans, leaves for maternity where applicable, and other benefits. Such an item as overtime provision can be very important when making salary comparisons. Some communities have evolved various arrangements to encourage and reward high education. The job seeker is well advised to inquire about tuition payment plans, as well as tuition reimbursements and, as mentioned elsewhere, any salary incentives for educational attainments.

As unions and collective bargaining units have entered into governmental work, indications are that fringe considerations, working conditions, and specific benefits are now all a part of employee-employer negotiation and contract.

There are other potential costs and expenses which are important to ascertain prior to deciding upon an agency. In some cases, all equipment and uniforms are furnished; in others the officer may have to purchase these. In some circumstances, the individual may be responsible for obtaining a weapon; in others, weapon, ammunition, holster, and leather belting may all be furnished. Good career planning requires that anyone review all of these various factors, since many young recruits are not in a position to make heavy initial monetary outlays in order to obtain a job.

Many people feel that one of the greatest advantages of a police career is the regularity and security of employment, particularly in times of economic instability. This security doubtless has attracted applicants over the years and will always appear attractive, especially when coupled with the early retirement age and the resulting pension. Many employees, notably those who entered law enforcement careers following World War II and the Korean War, have retired and pursued productive work in second careers. These second careers have ranged from industrial and retail security to college teaching and practicing law. Like military careers, law enforcement offers the advantage of a lifetime pension while one is young enough to engage in further vocational interests; yet also as in the military, many individuals remain in law enforcement because promotions have created new opportunities.

In either case, the retirement fund is a forced savings account at an attractive interest rate, and it is usually more than matched by the employer. This fund also assures an income in case of early retirement because of disability, and it provides family benefits in case of premature death. Although it may be true that one's greatest concern should not be his ultimate retirement, it is nonetheless accurate to say that law enforcement compares very favorably to other occupations in that regard.

OTHER INCENTIVES

One of the strongest attractions the police service holds for a young person is the opportunity to rise through the ranks. While this opportunity varies considerably, depending on the size of the department and personnel turnover, it is still something that most ambitious officers seek, because promotion brings higher pay, additional responsibility, and greater prestige. Because most promotions are made from within the organization and almost always occur after the individual has served several years in a particular rank, few outsiders are found in supervisory and command positions. Although enforcement agencies do employ chiefs or commissioners who have not previously served in the organization, the general pattern has been that those at the top have worked their way up through the ranks.

The procedure for advancement generally requires a written examination followed by an oral interview. The federal agencies often include a group interview in order to observe each candidate in a leadership situation. A medical examination often is required prior to promotion.

It is at promotion time when evidence in support of higher education is quite visible. Those officers with solid field experience now have the opportunity to respond to questions that are often gathered from standard textbooks and the current literature. Thus, the advantage should be with those who have studied formally, know good operating procedures, legal cases, what techniques are considered to be the state-of-the-art, and can communicate their responses in a clear and concise manner. Likewise, in an oral interview, a potential supervisor and commander should be exact and articulate, positive and yet reasonable, decisive and yet sensitive to others. These traits can be greatly enhanced when one possesses the self-confidence and good judgment that higher education encourages.

The development of Assessment Centers for promotion is considered a promising sign that a greater objectivity and more equitable measuring tool is at hand. Within the assessment process, the promotional candidate is asked to respond to several situations, role-play in a given scenario, and demonstrate what actions would be taken to meet a particular challenge. Trained assessors, predominately command officers, but also civilians, evaluate the candidate's performance in these simulated situations. This process, along with other tests and interviews, becomes a factor in deciding upon promotions. There have been some very fine examples of assessment centers selecting candidates for police chief and other command level positions in recent years, and more are to be expected. Business and industry have pioneered the assessment process, along with the federal government, including the FBI. Considering the investment in promoting personnel to top management positions, the expense of defining the tasks to be measured, developing the exercises, and training the assessors would seem quite justified.

The other feature considered in promotion is the system of seniority, which provides points for years of service wihin the agency. In recent years, the seniority system has decreased in favor of the written and oral performances. In the federal agencies, because of the salary scale, it is not as critical that one obtain a promotion in order to receive a pay raise.

In local and state agencies, aside from normal steps or increments, the salary scale is closely aligned to a military rank system, such as, corporal, sergeant, lieutenant, captain, and so on. Therefore, promotions are necessary in order to advance to the higher salaries in this field.

In the past few years, opportunities for promotion through lateral entry have been occurring. In other words, a promising and competent senior officer in one department might be offered the job of chief of police in a neighboring community. Moreover, a state police officer or a federal agent could be appointed as a police administrator in an agency other than the one in which prior career experience was obtained.

The important qualities in promotion are nor unlike those in any leadership role: sensitivity, directing others, good judgment, dependability, self-confidence, ability to delegate authority, persuasiveness, skill in communicating and motivating others. One of the most important contributions made by higher education in the law enforcement field has been the intellectual improvement of officers so that they are better equipped to succeed in promotional examinations. One must recognize, too, that most enforcement agencies have requirements relating to the number of years which must be served in a particular rank before one is eligible to complete for the next higher rating. This is not necessarily a serious restriction, since the years that are required have been reduced gradually as training and education became more acceptable in lieu of lengthy experience. Then too, law enforcement is a young person's occupation, and there is considerable opportunity for upward movement due to early retirements and second careers.

Of course, it is virtually impossible to predict what anyone's particular chances are for reaching a top position-that of a police chief or a sheriff or state police commissioner. Many individuals have achieved these positions with relatively few years in patrol and investigative assignments. Their appointments were based largely upon the leadership and administrative talents they demonstrated in the lower ranks. Also, recognizing that top positions are generally the direct result of political appointment or election, as in the case of the sheriff, many persons would prefer to achieve a command position where they have direct responsibility for the delivery of services, remaining there for the duration of their career.

In summary, what have we determined about police officer starting salaries, and the larger question, salaries to be reached over a two or three year period into the career? We can say with certainty that police salaries exceed those of most other public servants and certain professionals whose credentials have traditionally required higher education. Police officers have higher salaries than do crime lab technicians, probation and parole officers, private sector security officers, correctional officers, and case workers. Traditionally, in many local communities, police and fire fighter salaries have been linked; partly because the recruitment pool was similar, and partly due to these two positions being supported from the same public safety share of the tax dollar. In situations where the law enforcement salaries are ahead of fire service, it may be due to the higher education incentive monies available to police, or it may come about due to stronger mandated state standards and certification.

In the federal law enforcement agencies, described elsewhere in this book, salaries tend to be higher than in local and state government, and this becomes specially true after one attains several years of experience.

For the most part, anyone seeking employment within the federal system will become a part of the Government Service (GS) pay schedule. This system provides for annual pay steps and generally such employees progress one step up the GS scale after each year of service. Agencies vary as to entrance level because of the differences in qualifications, duties, and specialization required. However, most federal officers will be within several of the GS categories described in the following examples.

Let us consider a GS 7 who begins employment with the Drug Enforcement Administration. This special agent applicant would typically possess a Bachelor's degree and perhaps graduate level study too. If not graduate study, then some investigative experience will be required. The GS 7 can expect to currently earn $17,138 to start; in five years, that same agent would be earning $19,422 on the latest pay schedule. Many federal agents may receive overtime pay, sometimes as much as 25% of salary. They can generally assume that with travel, extended daytime duty, weekends and such that overtime will occur.

A GS 9 position typically requires not only the Bachelor's degree, but graduate study or a law degree, and as much as five years of significant investigative experience. The GS 9 starts at $20,965, and using our average agent example again, after five years, would be earning a base salary of $23,761. Top step on the GS 9 scale, schieved after 10 years service is $27,256.

In terms of career advancement, we might consider a GS 11 who headed a district administrative area and had a dozen years of service. An estimated salary for that manager would be about $33,000. For someone higher in the administrative structure, say a GS 12 with seniority, the salary would reach $40,000. Reviewing this further, it is easy to see how a senior supervisor, with overtime, and normal step progressions would expect to be earning up to $40,000, without necessarily having passed 40 years of age.

Pay raises with the federal government have been around the 4% figure in recent years, but that fluctuates according to the economy. Also, it is worth noting that all federal government employees hired now come under the Social Security Act.

Other federal service job benefits are equally attractive; there is often travel, quite extensive at times and the possibility does exist for transfer; and one of the better retirement systems available in the employment world, sometimes with provisions for retirement as early as age 50 after 20 years in certain types of assignments and agencies. In fact, retirement at age 50 has become more the rule than the exception with federal agents. Other normal fringes include paid vacation and holidays; low cost medical and life insurance; sick leave and financial protection for injury in the line of duty; and special federally supported death benefits. Federal service also affords a measure of employment security that is important to many.

Before concluding the discussion on service with the United States government, we should note that for those who reach the top of the agency structure, be they administrators appointed by the President, or deputy or assistant administrators, the earnings can reach $66,000. The range for a GS 15, for example, is presently from $50,252 up to $65,327.

We have now reviewed many of the factors associated with considering a career in terms of the rewards. Each aspirant must weigh goals and objectives with the many other considerations and think in terms of a career plan. Law enforcement, unlike most other occupations, offers two choices; that of a steady and long term commitment with relatively early retirement, or a shorter duration of active duty followed by numerous other endeavors that span only the imagination. Consider the ultimate example: joining a police department or a federal agency at age 21, then retiring after twenty years and serving in Congress, practicing law, or pursuing a new business, for an additional second career of another twenty years or more!

The concept of a *career development plan* is one which is receiving widespread attention and some implementation in modern law enforcement organizations. While not entirely a new idea, the actual use of such a plan in most criminal justice agencies is rather recent. For many years, the military and most federal departments have offered employees a career development approach which embraced special training, varying assignments, and opportunities to be rewarded and achieve recognition according to individual desire and capability.

In years past, local career development plans were quite informal and individual in nature, but have resulted in many former law enforcement officers leaving their original agency and moving on to become public safety director, college professors, heads of private security operations, as well as judges, legislators, and even mayors. This mobility factor strongly suggests to the young career aspirant that other alternatives will come one's way when an entry job is combined with formal education, relevant training opportunities, determination to succeed, and willingness to always consider carefully such new options. Preparing for one's retirement, and a second career is a very unique feature of working in criminal justice.

FRUSTRATIONS

Dedicated service to others can be very demanding, and police officers are among those who must perform their duties under conditions that are not always comfortable. Nor can such a career be regarded as one that is merely routine. All jobs, of course, have disadvantages, so whatever occupation is chosen, one can expect to endure some of the problems related to long hours, difficulties in getting ahead, daily frustrations, and disappointments. However, most law enforcement officers must contend with the rotation of shifts, and regardless of experience, it is never psychologically or physiologically easy to start the day's work at midnight. Stress has become a job-related illness which law enforcement administrators and psychologists are making efforts to alleviate and prevent. Many agencies now offer their employees a training program which involves advice on nutrition, exercise, and stress-reduction techniques.

Then, too, few occupations are as demanding on the emotions or as conflicting to one's logic and sense of reason as police work. Behind many of the daily difficulties of such a career lies a phenomenon which can rarely to comprehended, yet with which the officer must learn to live. This condition is *public apathy*. Its causes are numerous, but unfortunately, all those employed within the criminal justice system feel its impact. The public reflects its apathy through limitations of funds, lack of continuous support, indifference to the causes of crime, refusal to cooperate with authorities, and a frequent disinterest in the police as a unit of government and society.

This same public apathy translates itself to the police officer in the form of political leaders who fail to stand behind enforcement actions, a public which demands equal compliance with the law but expects personal immunity, and lastly, the loss os personal idealism which occurs to those who are sworn to uphold all laws, only to discover that citizens really expect something less of them.

THE ELEMENT OF DANGER

An element of danger always exists in the life of a peace officer, and there is certainly ample evidence that physical attacks on officers have increased in recent years. However, the advantages of challenge and excitement and the opportunity to prominently engage in such a vast array of circumstances, often outdoors, outweigh the physical risks in the minds of dedicated guardians of the peace. But

Police officers must use the utmost caution when stopping a suspect's vehicle.
Photo: James Stinchcomb.

there is still every reason to admit that any confrontation with people under stress, whether in a family quarrel or at a holdup scene, is a potentially dangerous one that calls for courage, both physical and emotional.

Anyone considering a career in law enforcement must recognize that, as the visible symbol of authority in the community, he or she may become the target of those choosing to resist, react against, or undermine established order. And while one admits to the ever-present danger and risk, the statistics also suggest that considering the many thousands of daily encounters between police and the public, relatively few end in injury or loss of life. Training and determined professional bearing are elements that equip the officer to deal with hazardous situations. The fact that many police injuries and deaths occur through traffic accidents, stopping vehicles whose occupants are unknown, and domestic arguments is strong evidence that thorough training and disciplined caution are essential. During 1982, 92 law enforcement officers were feloniously killed in the line of duty; ninety-one were killed in 1981, the year with the lowest number of job related deaths during the past decade. Assaults on officers continue to be a severe problem and call for extreme caution and careful attention on the part of any police officer dealing with an unknown situation. But to repeat, keep these losses in context and recognize that 24 hours of every day, police officers are in contact with every imaginable circumstance in their community.

As previously mentioned, a police officer must constantly deal with human suffering, but, unlike other citizens, the officer cannot permit personal emotions to take control. The requirements of the job demand that one always maintain self-control, act with calm efficiency, and display confidence and courage-while at the same moment not every appearing to lack compassion. No matter what is done, the officer cannot escape the fact that difficulty and tragedy must be faced daily, and no matter how hard one may try, the police are often unable to prevent them. This dilemma constitutes the emotional burden of a police officer's work, where safety is always at stake.

One must always recognize and understand that openly visible public support varies for the police according to the real level of concern that citizens have for the particular laws being enforced. There exists full public cooperation and support for police actions surrounding the kidnapping of a child; less but increasing amounts for drunken driving stops; and minimal, if any, support for strict enforcement of the laws prohibiting gambling.

Defensive tactics are a critical part of the recruits' curriculum, especially the techniques used in disarming an assailant. Photo: Miami-Dade Community College.

CHAPTER 6

EDUCATIONAL REQUIREMENTS

In recent years there has been a determined effort on the part of local governmental officials to demand that all police applicants be high school graduates. According to the President's Crime Commission (1967), more than 70 percent of the nation's police departments required the high school diploma as a requisite for employment. Beyond that, police departments in nine states and more than 30 departments in California alone had raised their standards to require some successful completion of college work. The state of California, effective in 1970, announced that six college credits would be required of all future peace officers employed within that state. Other enforcement agencies in such diverse locations as Flint, Michigan; Wichita, Kansas; Arlington, Virginia; Madison, Wisconsin; Bellvue, Washington; Dallas, Texas; and the Washington and Texas Highway Patrols have been giving priority to the completion of two years of college for entrance. Moreover, there are further indications that a number of major police agencies will move beyond the associate degree requirement, particularly for specialized, technical, and command positions.

It can be predicted safely that the future will call for some satisfactory college study prior to entrance into police service. Part of the reasoning for this statement lies in the fact that more and more young people will be attending colleges, particularly local community colleges, in the coming decades, and even if law enforcement were not to actively recruit from such sources, there would be a gradual tendency to attract all new personnel with exposure to higher education. Moreover, in 1973, the National Advisory Commission on Criminal Justice Standards and Goals recommended that, by 1982, every police agency should require a four-year college degree as a condition of initial employment. This projection was given considerable impetus by the fact that over 400 community and junior colleges offer associate degree programs in this career field, and beyond the associate level, there are a significant number of universities which now permit one to pursue a bachelor's degree in police administration, corrections, or criminal justice. (See the listing of colleges in Appendix C). The projections and national recommendations were made at a time when employment and economic conditions looked favorable; with inflation and the hiring limits imposed by pressures elsewhere, the academic requirements have been slowed but there is much evidence that higher education has become commonplace within police departments, and most major communities can expect to have a number of recruits with college backgrounds from now on.

Graduate degrees in criminal justice are becoming increasingly available and may be obtained specifically in law enforcement or in the related academic fields of public administration, criminology, or corrections. The growing availability of two-year, four-year, and graduate programs in law enforcement supports earlier statements regarding the importance of considering college preparation prior to entering criminal justice service at the local, state, or federal level.

Costs for the various programs in institutions of higher learning vary significantly. Generally speaking, the local community college is less expensive for students residing within that area; the state colleges and the state universities cost somewhat more. The out-of-state student will, of course, pay more to attend any of these institutions. The best procedure regarding tuition costs is to obtain a school catalog, and, if distance permits, to get an appointment with the director of the college criminal justice program. In cases where no specific law enforcement or corrections degree program is available, the prospective student should contact the general counselors in the institution about an appropriate course of study.

For persons who do not have access to a specialized degree program, related areas of study might include public administration, sociology, political science, and psychology, computer science, and business management.

HIGH SCHOOL

Some particular subjects in the high school curriculum will prove useful to one considering a career in general public service and, specifically, in law enforcement. They include American Government, civics, sociology, psychology, and social problems, as well as any other courses that deal with the social and human institutions in our society. Such a student might also be encouraged to pursue mathematics to develop deductive reasoning powers. Laboratory sciences that teach the importance of observation, recording, and accurate reporting are also helpful. The communications arts, learned through the study of writing, literature, and public speaking, are very important. In high schools where business law or other legal subjects are available, the law enforcement career aspirant would be well advised to begin to study this very important information. In addition, some police officers find skill in typing to be most useful. With the addition of computers into most agencies, a working knowledge of that field will also become advantageous. There are also some high schools now that offer a course in the Criminal Justice or Law Enforcement field; by all means, anyone with such a career inclination should take such a course.

COLLEGE

A student nearing completion of high school should obtain a catalog from several community colleges or universities offering a criminal justice degree in order to become familiar with specific entrance requirements. Some of these institutions will require that potential law enforcement majors demonstrate qualifications beyond that of simply possessing a high school diploma. While it is not generally regarded as desirable that the college establish rigid physical requirements for entrance into these specialized programs, it is important that students recognize the requirements of physical, character, and background investigations conducted by police agencies before an applicant is employed. Students should be reminded that successful completion of a college degree in law enforcement does not necessarily guarantee employment as a sworn police officer in the agency of one's choice. For this reason, there exist variations throughout the country with regard to admission to college programs.

Described below is a suggested balanced curriculum for both law enforcement and corrections associate degree students. These curricula represent revisions of those prepared by the author several years ago under a Kellogg Foundation Grant to the American Association of Community and Junior Colleges. They have been altered slightly to accommodate recent trends within community colleges and the criminal justice career field.

LAW ENFORCEMENT CURRICULUM SUMMARY

(Associate Degree)

First Year	*Second Year*
General Education Courses: English/Technical Report- writing Psychology Sociology/Criminology Government	General Education Courses: Math Humanities/Social Science
Technical, Specialized Courses: Introduction to Law Enforce- ment/Criminal Justice Police Organization/Admini- stration/Operations/ Procedures Juvenile Delinquency Preven- tion/Procedures/Control Criminal Law	Technical, Specialized Courses: Police Supervision Criminal Investigation Law of Evidence (Procedure) Police Community Relations/ Human Relations Introduction to Criminalistics Internship/Practicum/Field Experience Seminar

Most typical additional specialized courses include:
Traffic Administration/Control/Regulation
Administration of Justice (Emphasis on Courts and Legal Process)
Narcotics/Drug Abuse/Investigation
Minority/Race/Ethnic Relations

The associate degree program in corrections is presented for those persons interested in working with offenders and being a part of the treatment and rehabilitation process. (For details see Chapter 7.)

CORRECTIONS CURRICULUM SUMMARY

(Associate Degree)

First Year

General Education Courses:
English/Technical Report-
writing
Psychology
Sociology/Penology
Government
Technical, Specialized Courses:
Introduction to Corrections
Correctional Institutions
Juvenile Delinquency/Procedures
Criminal Law/Judicial Process

Second Year

General Education Courses:
Math
Humanities/Social Science
Abnormal Psychology/Collective
or Deviant Behavior
Technical, Specialized Courses:
Correctional Administration
Interviewing/Counseling
Community-based Corrections/
Treatment/Rehabilitation
Probation and Parole
Internship/Practicum/Field
Experience
Seminar

Most typical additional specialized courses include:
Administration of Justice (Emphasis on Courts and Legal Process)

Again, it is worth repeating here that communications skills should be mastered at the community college level for those preparing for university level study. Likewise, a community college student should take advantage of courses in the social and behavioral sciences in order to better understand the problems, stresses, and dilemmas encountered by the justice system and its representatives.

Bachelor's Degree in Administration of Justice/Criminal Justice

To begin planning for study at the university level, one should first obtain catalogs from those institutions that offer the specialized program with the appropriate balance of academic preparation in related fields of study. Persons with higher education find that opportunities arise as their careers progress, and it is always sound advice to obtain some knowledge base beyond that of the specialized major. Thus, the law enforcement (police) major may look to business management and computer science for electives or even a minor field of study; the corrections major would do something similar in fields related to human behavior and problem solving through counseling and other social work skills; the juvenile justice specialization might study further in rehabilitation or educational areas in order to augment a future career.

Many faculty members feel strongly that a criminal justice major, broadly based, is an excellent preparation for later law school study, social work, or public administration. Obviously, of course, if the career goal is in the criminalistics field, that is the science of laboratory examinations or research, then an entirely different type of undergraduate preparation is called for. Probably one in chemistry, biology or physics with strong preparation in mathematics and computers. An undergraduate major in the administration of justice should assist the university student in developing knowledge, abilities, and skills required for the demands of an effective practitioner.

Before selecting a Bachelor's program one should determine that it is going to provide a well-rounded knowledge of the discipline and the specialty which is desired. This means that the curriculum must address underlying concepts, theories, and principles but also present the state of the art in terms of practice. The program must also prepare the student to address problems and complex issues, to employ proper research skills, and to ultimately be able to apply techniques toward evaluating, analyzing and snythesizing issues which confront the field.

Assuming that the university student transfers from a community college where some specialization has been available, and that the fundamentals have already been received, then listed below are suggestions for an upper division academic experience. Of course, if the university student enters the senior institution as a freshman, courses to be taken would still involve the Introductory ones, Criminal Law, Investigation, and some of the others mentioned previously. (Areas of study listed below are meant to be descriptive of the subject and not necessarily course titles.)

LAW ENFORCEMENT (POLICE) OPTION OR SPECIALIZATION

Administration, Planning & Management
Economic Offenses/Organized Crime
Industrial & Retail (Private) Security
Theories and Practices in Police Agencies
Strategies for Crime & Delinquency Prevention
Case Studies in Legal Evidence & Procedures
Criminalistics & Crime Analysis
Human Behavior in Criminal Justice

CORRECTIONS (TREATMENT AND REHABILITATION)

Administration (Adult & Juvenile)
Community Based Corrections Programming
Correctional Law
Evaluation & Treatment of Offenders
Counseling & Therapeutic Techniques

JUVENILE JUSTICE

Juvenile Justice Law & Process
Strategies for Crime & Delinquency Prevention
Courses related to Behavior, Treatment, &
    Administration cited above

In addition to the specialization courses, there are common core ones which reflect information necessary for anyone entering the justice system with a Bachelor's degree. These might be described as follows:

Courts and Judicial Process
Crime and Delinquency Prevention

Criminal Justice Research
Comparative Justice Systems
Critical Issues or Topic Seminars
Field Experience/Internships

Additional upper division skills, not necessarily obtained solely through criminal justice departments, but clearly relevant to career planning, are:

Research & Evaluation Techniques
Policy Analysis and Public Administration
Information Systems
Accounting and Auditing Procedures
Counseling & Treatment Techniques

One majoring in the Criminal Justice body of knowledge should consider a minor field of study in such departments or programs as Sociology, Psychology, Urban Planning, Public Administration, Social Work, Political Science, Computer Sciences, or Business Management and Information Systems. Again, for the laboratory major, the minors would be from the physical sciences and mathematics. Emerging specializations which are justice related can be found in more and more colleges and universities. These might include fire safety and fire science; private security and loss prevention; traffic and transportation safety; and there are degrees entirely devoted to safety; occupational, home, and recreational. An excellent combination of such programs can be found in some state universities, and a student might consider a combination of majors among justice related and safety related fields. For those considering law school, a possible direction might be to mix justice and safety topics with government and business studies. Before final decision making a serious student might do well to obtain some catalogs from well-established and well-recognized universities in this field. Seek out their course descriptions and options for combining areas and then proceed according to what such programs as these would provide in breadth. Depending upon the location of the country which appeals to you, some of these broadly based curricula can be found at the following institutions of higher learning:

Eastern Kentucky University

Southern Illinois University
Michigan State University
Sam Houston State University
Virginia Commonwealth University
Indiana University
Florida State University
American University
California State University-Fresno
California State University-Sacramento
California State University-Long Beach
Central Missouri State University
University of Maryland
Northeastern University
University of Nebraska-Omaha
John Jay College of Criminal Justice

Many more than those named above offer criminal justice, but by reviewing catalogs and program options from some with comprehensive programs, a student can begin to see the potentials for a career. One might want to combine public sector and private sector courses; another might wish to combine legal and investigative courses with fire safety and fire protection; still another student could mix traffic safety with research and analysis; while another may want a more traditional law enforcement emphasis but with additional studies in laboratory procedures and crime scene analysis. Review the catalogs and then discuss the possibilities with faculty advisors, family members, and very importantly, with persons who are currently employed in various aspects and levels of the justice and safety systems.

In every state now there are also graduate degree programs; one can obtain a Master's Degree (30-36) credits with concentrations in policy, administration, research, or in areas related to correctional treatment. Persons with graduate training typically enter teaching, research, mid-level management, and some of the newer occupations involving planning, project direction, and organizational analysis. Doctorates are also available in Public Administration, Criminology, and Criminal Justice, all of which generally lead to teaching and research.

CADET PROGRAM—A WORK-STUDY PLAN

The cooperative training aspects of many occupational education programs have, for the most part, not yet been included in law enforcement programs. Instead, on-the-job training has been provided for pre-service students through informal arrangements which frequently are worked out between the police student and the law enforcement agency. The absence of large numbers of formal work-study arrangements probably results from hesitance on the part of the community college to involve students in which is perceived as a potentially hazardous experience.

In any event, most law enforcement educational programs do not yet provide work experience as a part of the formal educational process. However, there are some students who gain law enforcement experience during their college careers through full or part-time employment with a local agency as a records clerk, typist, or other civilian employee. Such work experience is rarely assessed and bears little ressemblance to the carefully supervised and evaluated internship period associated with other occupational programs.

It is essential, then, that greatly expanded law enforcement work experience programs be established in the future. The community college can make a significant contribution to such programs because of its proximity to occupational life in the community. Community colleges can help the student get on-the-job experience that makes classroom work realistic and increase motivation. In addition to these advantages to the individual, work programs assure that the college curricula is being tested each day in the actual work environment. Through the combined efforts of such organizations as the International Association of Chiefs of Police and the American Association of Community and Junior Colleges, a dramatic increase in work experience programs in law enforcement is forecast in the years ahead.*

Guidelines for Work Experience Programs in the Criminal Justice System, by Jimmy C. Styles and Denny F. Pace. American Association of Community and Junior Colleges, 1 Dupont Circle, Washington, D.C. 20036.

The concept of the *police cadet* is by no means a recent phenomenon, and, in fact, the program now appears to be gaining momentum throughout the nation. The basic purpose of police cadet programs is to facilitate police recruiting by making it possible to employ selected youths aged 17 to 19 who demonstrate superior potential for police careers, but who are unable to be recruited because of the minimum age requirement.

In some communities they have been given titles as Community Service Officer, or Public Safety Aides, but the concept is to assist young people to enter related careers early and to gain experience while attending college. The medical field and various high technology areas of industry do this regularly, and the process provides for a steady flow of motivated and educated persons into an occupational specialty.

Many large cities, including New York City, Chicago, Miami, Washington, D.C., Detroit, Baltimore, New Orleans, and St. Louis, have established such programs and generally report considerable satisfcation with them. The cadet program is not at all limited to the large city. Smaller communities also have manpower requirements which can be met by persons not possessing sworn police powers. Since this publication cannot possibly list the large number of such communities, the young career aspirant is urged to contact department administrators within his region to learn whether such an opportunity exists. Described below are examples of specific police cadet programs.

Chicago Police Department. About three-fourths of police cadets are serving in districts, assisting sergeants in clerical capacities. The remainder are scattered throughout the Bureau of Staff Services, with a few in the Office of the Superintendent and the Bureau of Inspectional Services. Although job experience is an important part of a training program, cadets are productive employees who are expected to fully earn their salaries.

Most cadets work the second watch to permit regular attendance of college classes. A condition of employment is that each cadet must enroll for a minimum of 6 semester hours in police-oriented courses at an accredited college or university.

They work, they attend classes, they play basketball on their own teams in the police department league, they look forward to the day they can qualify for appointments as patrol officers. They have the potential, individually and as a group, to make important contributions to the department. The program keeps them involved in police procedures through the critical years between graduation from high school and their 21st birthdays.

Detroit Civil Service Commission. Cadets work in accordance with departmental policies and procedures and the provisions of a departmental training program. They are subject to specific assignment and instruction as well as frequent review of work by supervisors. Trainees participate in a departmental program of instruction in modern police methods and duties, and perform a variety of miscellaneous pre-patrol duties. They also are responsible for performing a variety of such routine clerical duties as typing, filing, and preparing police forms and records; operating a private branch exchange telephone switchboard and recording hourly calls from and relaying instructions to street patrol officers; maintaining records of all arrest and missing persons; recording change of address for vehicle operators' licenses.

San Diego Police Department. Cadets work a full 40-hour week at their departmental jobs. Their work is a form of training, inasmuch as they are learning departmental procedures and are becoming acquainted with key departmental personnel as a part of their jobs. Cadets are rotated among various assignments at six-month intervals to become familiar with many aspects of departmental operations.

In addition, cadets, are required to carry six units per semester in police science or related subjects at San Diego Junior College. This training is to be accomplished on their own time before or after regular working hours.

Cadets are required to furnish and wear a uniform that is very similar to that worn by the regular departmental officers. The cost of the uniform is borne by the cadet.

When they reach age twenty-one, cadets are eligible to take a promotional examination for advancement to police patrol status. A "promotional" eligible list takes priority over the "open" eligible list regularly used in filling police patrol positions. Thus, all successful cadets should be able to become police patrol officers as soon as they reach the necessary age.

RECRUIT TRAINING

All newly appointed law enforcement officers receive some form of initial training prior to being assigned to their duties. In general, it can be said that those recruits in the federal, state, and metropolitan jurisdictions are assigned to an organized training program that may vary in length from eight-to-ten weeks up to six months. New officers in smaller communities may not have equal opportunity to obtain as much preparation for service, although most are permitted to enroll in academies that are operated by the large cities or the state agency. Fortunately, new statewide training courses are being made available to more officers than ever before-in some places through the junior and community college systems, and in other places through regionally distributed academy facilities.

As state minimum standards legislation now exists everywhere, it can finally be said of local and state officers that they must attain whatever certification is required. Thus, whether the training be offered in their own department, in a regional academy, or in a centralized state setting, all states have some form of minimum requirement and curriculum which must be successfully completed. The number and content of minimum required recruit training hours still varies, some as low as 120-160 and some as high as 300-360, or even 400 but these are only minimums and they bring with them the important message that professional status for sworn law enforcement officers is rapidly arriving.

Beyond requirements for recruit training, new emphasis is being placed upon supervisory development so that those promoted to sergeant will have a thorough knowledge of their jobs. In the mid-

dle management ranks, such as lieutenant, it is vital that new instruction be offered, because patrol and investigative experiences
cannot prepare one sufficiently for command assignments. And officials in the top command positions, regardless of street experience, require training in budgeting, planning, and effecting
organizational efficiency. No easy method exists for delivering all
this necessary knowledge to the various assignments, and so we find
that a variety of training courses is available, but not necessarily
equally throughout the nation.

Although recruit training curricula vary among the local and state
agencies, particularly with regard to local ordinances, use of departmental equipment and report forms, and policies pertaining to local
rules and regulations-all of them include lectures on first aid, investigation, traffic control, patrol procedures, laws of arrest, and
courtroom conduct and testimony. The new officer also can expect
to spend time on the firing range and in the gymnasium in order to
become proficient in the use of weapons and self-defense.

There is a great deal to be taught and very little class time for it
all, so schedules are strict, complete note-taking generally is required, and a disciplined atmosphere may prevail. Some departments now are rescheduling their recruit training to give the new officer an opportunity for field experience in conjunction with
classroom study.* In recent years, there has been an increase in the
number of non-police personnel employed by police academies,
although the majority of lecturers are law enforcement personnel.
Those experienced personnel from the agency itself are able to bring
considerable background to the course they instruct, while holding
operating costs to a minimum. Guest lecturers are, however, very
essential. They come from federal agencies, the courts, and a variety of local agencies with which the police regularly deal.

Some examples of guest lecturers who could be considered critical
to the police training experience would be attorneys from the prosecution office, arson investigators from the fire department, in-

---

Law Enforcement Training and the Community College, by Denny F.
Pace, James D. Stinchcomb, and Jimmie C. Styles. American Association
of Community and Junior Colleges, 1 Dupont Circle, N.W., Washington,
D.C. 20036 (1970).

vestigators from the medical examiners office and commanders of special units such as helicopter, canine, tactical or swat, and the like.

Local community colleges and universities frequently have assisted police academies by offering instruction on such material as criminology, delinquency, psychology, report writing, human behavior, communications, and other academic topics relating to police work. The future will see academic preparation being incorporated into police training and an increase in the opportunity to obtain college credits for studies in the recruit training program.

Most police training includes some exposure to audio-visual techniques and training films. This is because new officers must have the opportunity to observe as much as possible before facing real-life situations. To that end, they may be required to demonstrate automobile driving habits, participate in a simulated crime scene search, testify in a mock trail, and practice such skills as lifting fingerprints and taking photographs. The grading system varies among departments, but tests occur regularly, and students who do not show promise of success can expect to be dropped from the academy. Their grades, along with later efficiency ratings, become a part of their permanent personnel record.

State and federal training programs for recruits are often longer than those for local agencies. They also probably reflect better facilities and more budget for this important purpose. Of course, the material is designed to accommodate the needs of the particular organization, so that highway patrol officers will focus greater attention on the motor vehicle code and accident investigation, while federal agents will concentrate on the statutes which will be their ultimate responsibility. All, however, have some aspects in common, such as defensive tactics, firearms usage, prisoner searches, handling of physical evidence, courtroom demeanor, and preparing accurate reports.

Depending upon the type and jurisdictional responsibility of the agency, they would also be exposed to considerable hours in the criminal and constitutional laws, community relations and citizen respect, handling of disturbances, proper radio procedures, basic investigations, and how to recognize and respond to various emergencies. Today's police recruits are also being informed as to their own needs in terms of mental health and stress reduction, and the importance of relaxation, positive outlook and good nutrition and exercise.

The modern police academy, whatever its duration and emphasis, places considerable priority on performance and one's ability to demonstrate that the tasks are understood and can be accomplished. Competency-based training, or performance-based training, as they are often termed by military schools, are the methods most likely to prove that a recruit is capable of actually saving a life through CPR or other procedure, and not simply answer a question about it on an exam in a classroom. To demonstrate the technique for stopping a vehicle, searching a premises, or removing an assailant's weapon, means more than writing about it. Through video-taping the exercises, and using simulated situations, the new officer obtains a realism previously unknown in the academy.

Again, depending upon the size of the jurisdiction, the minimum standards requirements of that state, and factors such as the agency's determination to prepare all new officers as much as possible, a police trainee might be required to complete as many as 800 to 1000 hours of basic subjects. It is not uncommon at all to locate situations where the state standards may dictate only 300 hours and the regional academy or the agency training bureau making two or three times that number available to newly employed recruits.

One state, Minnesota, has set standards that are quite progressive and has become, along with California and Florida, a pace setter in certification requirements. In Minnesota, officers must take at least two years of training, either through a vocational-technical program or in a college. Both academic subjects and required skills are covered. This has been in effect since 1977 and goes even beyond the basic course. Every three years, to maintain certification, the officer in Minnesota must complete another 48 hours of state-approved training. Some of the topics in recruit training have been mentioned previously, but let us look at what else one must learn prior to entering police service:

- The role of environmental protection agencies and how is pollution control enforced?

- What is the expectation of law enforcement in terms of ethics and standards of conduct? Legal terminology should be mastered, and not only statues and basic laws of arrest.
- Public Speaking, report writing, and non-verbal communications are all crucial.
- Sensitivity to various groups, be they minority, handicapped, elderly, or young and the many facets of drug abuse, alcoholism, and mental illness which one encounters.
- Firefighting and recognizing hazards and risks during routine patrol.
- Dealing with traffic problems, be they drunken drivers or congestion, or crashes.
- Interviewing and preliminary investigative techniques and procedures.
- Crisis intervention skills and proper approaches to calls for service.
- Use of the firearm, baton, handcuffs, and unarmed defense techniques.

Following completion of their formal classroom studies, most enforcement officers are assigned to work under the supervision of an experienced officer who must evaluate the new employee's performance periodically. In addition to a supervisor, the recruit may work with a more experienced partner for a period of time in order to receive instruction in specific methods and procedures and to ensure that all efforts are in line with departmental policy. Of course, the effectiveness of such procedures depends upon the personnel involved, but all departments agree on the importance of on-the-job training for recruits.

The probation period generally is regarded as having its beginning upon entrance into the recruit training program. It may continue for at least one year, and in some agencies, it lasts for 24 months. During that period, the new officer receives not only classroom instruction, but also field training and much initial on-the-job experience under supervision. This transition period is a critical one in terms of detecting deficiencies in the selection process as well as weaknesses in the classroom training program.

After the police recruit has worked under the guidance and supervision of the Field Training Officers, as they are often termed, he or she is eligible for full status as a patrol officer. But even then, performance evaluation continues to occur since from now on, it is no longer the classroom or the close supervision of the experienced officer to rely upon; only one's own judgement and decision making abilities.Most police administrators feel strongly that observing one's performance is the best way to evaluate whether or not the new recruit is suited for a police career. Such views are strongly supported by the fact that the stresses and conflicts of enforcement work cannot totally and adequately be simulated, and, therefore, one must perform duties before being assigned permanent status as a police officer.

In some agencies, the probation period is spent rotating from one major division to another in order to become acquainted with the entire organization. Ideally, performance ratings during the probation period will be frequent, classroom re-training will occur, and conferences with supervisors will be scheduled on a regular basis. In addition, as more effective training evaluation occurs, feedback from the recruits to the training academy is becoming increasingly important, in order to ensure the relevance of basic training to on-the-job needs.

Formal licensing and certification for law enforcement officers occurs when they are sworn in to their positions, take the oath of office and are awarded a badge. As mentioned previously, the state also then certifies them as having completed the required training and authorized to serve. The badge in all jurisdictions is, of course, the symbol of legal authority, and with it comes the power of detaining, arrest, and a number of other responsibilities for community safety and security. The uniform and badge also symbolize that one is the visible representative of government and authority and in a democracy this is a very important point to recognize when considering the implications of a career choice.

As state licensing standards increase, and higher education

becomes even more a part of police career development, the profession can be very proud of the early developments in California, under their Peace Officer Standards and Training Commission, which undertook the task of setting standards in the mid-1960's. At the same time both New York and New Jersey were enacting legislation of the same type, so it is accurate to state that law enforcement has had state legislation requiring certification and the meeting of training standards for over twenty years in some locales. In Florida now, more so than in any other state, there is a legal decertification process in practice as well for those who are found to not measure up to the expectations of agency regulation and state statute.

More and more too, the law officer is being offered in-service training at an advanced level to insure up-to-date knowledge and skills. Again, as with recruit training, states are beginning to mandate advanced courses for those who expect to be specialists or to be promoted. Most agencies have encouraged career development study in the past, even if it were conducted briefly and within the department itself.

The subjects may range from handling the mentally disturbed to recent court decisions, but the purpose is to keep officers current, alert, and informed. One of the most effective methods for giving in-service training to all officers is often termed "roll-call training." This technique, a 15-minute daily coverage of the practical aspects of policing, was offered in the Los Angeles Police Department in 1948. The information has been published in book form, and today these manuals are used in other police departments throughout the country.

In 1964, the International Association of Chiefs of Police began publishing a twice-monthly *Training Key*, available to all members of an agency at a very low cost and covering a variety of practical police subjects. Each issue deals with a specific topic, such as searching a suspect, handling the mentally ill, stopping a vehicle, and various first aid and investigative procedures. The *Training Key* has proven quite successful across the nation, since few departments could afford the research and production costs necessary to produce similar publications of their own.

There also are many opportunities to participate in specialized training through institutes and short courses. These may be provided by community colleges, universities, federal agencies, or by the local departments themselves. It is very important that officers assigned to certain specialties receive training that equips them to deal more effectively with their particular area of concern. Any specialized operation demands greater competence, and police officers cannot assume that their experience alone can provide that knowledge.

Certain courses that occur most frequently include those aimed at specialists in juvenile, vice, criminal investigation, traffic, and more recently, computer use, narcotics, community relations, and planning. In addition, there are programs for those who have the training responsibilities for their departments. A training calendar is provided monthly through the IACP's *Police Chief Magazine.* However, there are several agencies and institutions of higher learning which offer regular well-established programs varying in length from several weeks to several months.

The National Academy conducted by the Federal Bureau of Investigation is perhaps the most noteworthy of those programs conducted by federal agencies. This twelve-week session has been operating since the 1930s, and officers from throughout the fifty states as well as many foreign countries are selected to attend. The National Academy has had a significant percentage of its graduates become top level administrators in enforcement agencies over the years.

The Northwestern University Traffic Institute (1804 Hinman Avenue, Evanston, Illinois) affords a variety of specialized courses for enforcement personnel. The nine-month course is particularly concerned with traffic management and police administration. In addition to the long course, there are a number of two-and three-week sessions devoted to topics such as supervision, accident investigation, and traffic techniques.

The University of North Florida, in Jacksonville, operates The Institute of Police Traffic Management, and offers unique courses in resource management, budget planning, use of mini-computers, and other topics which are related to traffic, radar, motorcycles, and vehicular accidents and record analysis.

The University of Louisville (Louisville, Kentucky) has operated the Southern Police Institute for over two decades. Originally developed to assist officers throughout the southeast, it now accepts applicants from agencies throughout the nation. It also provides a variety of two-week programs with a special three-month course for in-service, supervisory, and command personnel.

The National Crime Prevention Institute, created in 1971 also operates from the School of Justice Administration at the University of Louisville and offers various courses for persons concerned with prevention and security.

Several federal agencies conduct specialized courses for local and state law enforcement officers. These include courses on narcotics investigation; hostage and terrorist tactics; explosives and bombs; and the like. Currently, many of these are available at the Federal Law Enforcement Training Center located in Glynco, Georgia. This is the setting where most federal agents receive training and it also offers specialty programs to other jurisdictions. The Glynco center does some particularly good work in high risk topics such as officer survival, executive protection, driver training and crash avoidance, hazardous materials and computer security.

Throughout the entire preceeding chapter we have considered the great importance of career preparation. Whether it be by considering one's high school electives, carefully selecting the department or agency that provides the most up-to-date training, and seeking out additional study opportunities, both through in-service, career-development training courses, and of course, through higher education, it is most important. The law enforcement community affords personnel numerous opportunities for one day or one week training and the wise employee looks ahead to these and seeks them out. Criminal Justice is too broad a field of endeavor, and includes too many new directions, for anyone to consider stopping after high school. The local community college, or the state university must be the next step in order to prepare properly for working with our social order. Law enforcement training gives one the organizational setting and the formal authority to take charge of situations and to make decisions that really count.

Volunteers at the Safer Foundation work with former prison inmates, offering counseling, basic skills education, and job counseling and placement. Photo: Safer Foundation.

CHAPTER 7

RELATED CAREERS IN CRIMINAL JUSTICE AND PUBLIC SAFETY

A number of career opportunities are available throughout the administration of justice and public safety systems. Although law enforcement is certainly the most visible and the phase that most citizens recognize, it is by no means the only vocation concerned with the problems of crime and delinquency. Because the police are instantly identified, and their actions are the most reported and commented about, it is no wonder that people thinking about careers focus upon that sector. The fact remains that many other jobs prevail throughout public safety, and this chapter will attempt to describe and assess them as logical alternatives.

To be sure, one's career goals require some early planning, and such factors as higher education, physical characteristics, personal determination, and often family and teacher advice will play a part in setting those directions. It is entirely likely that some of the readers of this book, while thinking about law enforcement generally, will want to seek out further information about the related endeavors as they are described. The student who is interested and successful in high school chemistry and physics should look at the world of criminalistics as it relates to an interest in crime solving. Likewise, the student interested in political science, logic, and government may prefer a career in criminal law. It is important to think of the justice and safety systems as an interlocking group of enterprises which have common goals. The paths one chooses to help our society to attain those goals may differ, just as many vocational choices exist within the wide variety of medical services. There are important choices to be made, and gathering accurate information is the first step.

This section will discuss law as a profession, with the specializations that affect the justice system directly; criminalistics and the forensic crime laboratory; the broad field of corrections and rehabilitation; and the increasing and fast-changing business of private security, loss reduction, and specialized protection services.

The practice of law in its many forms is perhaps the most obvious pursuit of a related career field. This book will have little to say about the legal profession, since there is available a publication on opportunities in law careers. Anyone who is thinking about law as a career would do well to obtain that publication.* However, we should note in this text that a number of legal officers are participants in the justice system, and it is not uncommon for persons working in criminal justice to obtain law training as well.

Let us quickly review the general career options one has when the law degree has been completed, still assuming that work in the justice system is the goal. State and local prosecution offices number over 8000; these are the agencies engaged in the prosecution of alleged criminal offenders, although some are also providing civil legal services to government. At the state level, these would include the Office of the Attorney General, states' attorneys, district attorneys, and prosecuting attorneys. The titles of county level prosecution officials are quite varied, but include county attorney, corporation counsel, county solicitors, and district attorney to name a few. In contrast, a relatively new law-related agency is the Office of the Public Defender; the smallest of all criminal justice sectors. Like the prosecutor, these offices are supported by public funds, with their responsibility deriving from one's constitutional right to legal counsel.

Three-fourths of all public defender offices are administered by county government, and less than one fourth by state government. The office of public defender is growing, and most public defenders now handle the full range of criminal cases, along with some civil

---

Opportunities in Law Careers, Gary A. Munneke. National Textbook Company, Lincolnwood, IL, 1981.

areas as well. Here again is a fine example of a career that relates to criminal law and offenders, but also services the needs of persons who seek legal assistance for housing, consumer, welfare and various domestic matters. Public defenders do not merely represent those charged with crimes.

There are about 17,000 courts, which represent the second largest sector of the justice system. Courts are agencies or units of the judicial branch of government which have authorization, by statute or constitution, to decide controversies and disputed matters of fact brought before them. There are appellate, general, and limited levels of court jurisdiction. All of these employ judges, clerks, and private practice attorneys. Some also have court administrators, another relatively new career, to oversee and supervise the process. A typical court administrator might be employed under the general direction of the chief judge to manage all administrative functions of that court. These functions would include directing a staff responsible for the processing of traffic, civil, and criminal cases, as well as providing court security and many other non-legal duties. Many positions exist for court administrators in the $30,000-$40,000 range, and graduate training in public administration or court administration is required. The future growth is promising, due to continuing state-level court reorganization plans and the backlogs in courts, which result in delays and political pressures to alleviate them.

Jobs for bailiffs, court officers and those other non-legal positions affiliated with court expansion are increasing. Both size and number of courts have increased in recent years, and that growth appears to be continuing. With it will continue the demand for maintaining order and the numerous other tasks of the bailiff and court officers. Other positions, such as law clerks, clerks of the court, legal, stenographers and legal transcribers also service the court system in a supportive capacity.

The court system is undergoing extensive change in this country, and the occupational situation is changing and improving. Not only are increased personnel to be expected, but greater specialization and newly-expanded duties as well.

Judges, who may serve in any number of different jurisdictional levels, basically listen to testimony, rule on what evidence may be acceptable, and either decide the case or instruct the jury on the law and their options for a decision. Numbers of judicial positions have been on the increase, again due to backlogs and increased criminal trials. There are district courts, juvenile and traffic courts, appeals courts, probate courts, municipal courts, and of course supreme courts. Nearly all judges now have legal training and extensive courtroom trial experience. Salaries will vary considerably according to the level of jurisdiction and responsibility. A salary of $80,000 to $90,000 would not be unusual for state and federal supreme court justices. In most jurisdictions, judges are elected for a specific term, although at the federal level, they are appointed for life. District-level judges would be paid in the range of $60,000; salaries would be less for those in municipal, juvenile, and other local courts. A local or municipal court judge could expect a salary from about $35,000 up to $60,000.

We have described briefly the main actors in the court and judicial process; other graduates of law schools are employed by government to research and prepare legislation. The police legal advisor has already been mentioned as a newly-emerging career for those lawyers who may wish to remain, or to become affiliated, with a police agency. Many political careers, and surely many judicial careers, are launched by first serving as the local prosecutor or county attorney. It should be clear that the lawyer, and more recently, the court administrator, are interwoven into the system, and many career opportunities are projected for their type of public service.

CORRECTIONS AND REHABILITIATION

This interesting, and sometimes overlooked, field encompasses a wide array of jobs. Depending upon one's personal interests and inclinations, a correctional worker can be found in an institutional setting as a uniformed correctional officer; with a probation office servicing needs of the non-institutionalized offender; as a caseworker whose clients require specialized attention; or as a correctional counselor dealing with the many problems and circumstances of the offender, whether institutionalized or not. Since institutions—from local county jails to large maximum security penitentiaries—all are communities within themselves, there are positions such as work supervisors, teachers, chaplains, medical personnel, psychologists, and many others, including of course, the command staff, most of whom began as sworn correctional officers.

As with police departments, correctional institutions are found at all levels of government. At the local level, one might seek employment in the jail, a stockade or workhouse, a women's facility, a regional center for youthful offenders, or a specialized facility, such as group homes dealing with addictions. Some local jail staff are employed initially as deputy sheriffs and cross-trained in order to serve as patrol deputies also.

Generally speaking, the correctional officer of today has progressed to where many possess some higher education, are trained to respond to emergencies and stiuations within their institutions, and have gradually become regarded as a part of the rehabilitative process in corrections. This might be especially true in the case of youthful offender facilities or those housing and treating juveniles.

The challenge of the correctional officer is to maintain security and safety of the inmate population, and at the same time, gain an acceptance and a trust that will assist the offender, in developing socially acceptable behavior when released back into the community. Those working in state and federal systems may expect transfer, especially upon promotion, and the salaries and benefits will vary greatly. Some correctional personnel are paid similar wage rates as deputy sheriffs in their jurisdiction; some are a part of collective bargaining units, with wages set according to negotiations with the unit of government; some are paid according to the prevailing salary scale throughout their system, as with the federal government.

According to the most recent data available from the U.S. Bureau of Justice Statistics, there are about 5700 correctional facilities within the grouping of local jails, state adult correctional institutions, and juvenile facilities. The vast majority of the local jails are "dependent", meaning that they are administered by a sheriff's department or police department. It is interesting to note that several states administer the jail system at the state level. These include Connecticut, Delaware, Rhode Island, Vermont, and Hawaii. Another interesting jail statistic is that nearly half of all jail inmates are housed in only 5% of the nation's jails. It is also vitally important to remember that some 40% of jail residents are unconvicted; meaning that they are either awaiting trial, or have not yet been arraigned. At the state level, one finds some 800 adult confinement and community-based facilities. These might include prisons, diagnostic and reception centers, drug or alcoholic treatment centers, prison farms, road camps, and community-based settings such as half-way houses, pre-release facilities and youthful offender institutions. By way of contrast, some 95% of inmates housed in state corrections systems are within the confinement facilities that are typically known as prisons; only some 5% are within settings described as community-based. Employment potential in community-based work in corrections is by no means universal; some states have no such programs, and several states, notably, Florida, Michigan, and Pennsylvania have many. All states, of course, have a major prison.

Listed among the 1100 publicly-operated juvenile facilities are detention centers, group homes, ranches, forestry camps, and training schools. Many are state-operated, but an equal number are county-administered; very few are at the city level. The largest numbers of specialized facilities for juveniles and youth are found in California, with New York and Ohio next. There has been a recent trend to increase the number of open and smaller facilities in order to focus more specialized treatment and attention on persons with the best hope for rehabilitation. Employment potential for working with youth is expected to continue to increase.

The work in corrections extends beyond the institution; some offenders leave the courtroom and are placed on probation which does not entail any form of confinement. Others, released after serving part of their sentence, are on parole. The positions of probation and parole will be discussed next.

Salaries vary greatly for correctional workers; sworn, uniform officers may range from starting levels around $15,000 to very large jurisdictions where the starting figure may be $18,000. With overtime and regular increases, an average correctional officer in this country might be earning close to $20,000. For probation and parole staffs, nearly all of whom are college graduates, the salaries reflect the local or state situations, and could be as modest as $15,000 for entry juvenile court counselor, or as high as $30,000 for an experienced parole supervisor. Much depends upon the type of agency one is serving.

Probation officers, sometimes called agents, have responsibility for compiling what is known as the pre-sentence investigation for the court. This officer may also be asked to make a formal court report and a recommendation to the judge for case disposition. In some locales, there are investigators who primarily conduct such investigations and compile the information for the probation officer. Regardless of the size and volume of the jurisdiction however, the probation officer is the professional who is responsible for advising and counseling the caseload of individuals that have been placed on probation by the court. This counseling includes personal matters, social adjustment, work and economic circumstances, and all areas that would influence the required adjustment of the offender. Probation work exists with both juveniles and adults; and in all cases a plan must be formulated for directing and enforcing an effective rehabilitation arrangement. Much of the work of a probation officer involves contact with family, employers, and others whose lives affect that of the person on probation. Anyone interested in probation as a career would usually possess a bachelor's degree in the social sciences, human behavior, or criminal justice. At the graduate level, a master's degree is often required for supervisory duties and promotion. That degree might be in social work, or in a field that relates closely to understanding and influencing human behavior.

Parole officers do much the same type of work, and have many of the same kinds of responsibilities. The difference is that their clientele have already served time in institutions, and have been released conditionally *on parole*. Hence, the parolee may require a more intensive supervision, and in some cases, group therapy and other behavior adjustment techniques are called for. The parole officer may have to make the actual arrangements for the client to have a place to live, a job, and may also have to enforce those arrangements under the conditions of the release.

There are various opportunities for advancement in both probation and parole; there are intensive case loads for therapy and counseling purposes; there are field supervisors and office managers and district or regional administrators. As stated earlier, these positions function at both federal and state levels, as well as local, county levels. They also service both juveniles, young adults, and adult offenders. There are institutional parole officers, whose tasks involve assisting the inmate prior to early release or supervise persons who are about to be released in their adjustment process. The work is challenging and rewarding. An excellent way to learn more about this field is to ask to perform an internship as part of the college educational experience. Many probation and parole offices welcome college students who can assist in conducting investigations, and in participating in basic offender supervision work.

As reported by the 1976 National Manpower Survey, there were about 220,000 persons employed in local, state, and federal correctional facilities and probation and parole offices.* The largest single group of employees in this system serves as *correctional officers* (in the past, commonly known as guards or custodial officers).

In addition to the primary responsibility of keeping offenders safely in custody, the correctional officer in recent years has come to be recognized as an important component of the treatment and rehabilitation process. With the limited availability of qualified treatment professionals, and in view of the close and continual contact between correctional officers and inmates, the role of the correctional officer in achieving successful rehabilitation is becoming increasingly evident. Assignments in this position vary according to the extent of contact with the inmates and the ype of institution (i.e., whether minimum or maximum security). But, duties would involve responsibility for security of the institution, control of con-

---

*Recent data in 1982 suggest that this figure has grown to something closer to 300,000 employees because of new institutions and increased inmate populations.

traband (non-permissible materials), and supervision and guidance of the many repair, maintenance, manufacturing, and other inmate work services-from clothing factories to farming operations. In addition, significant counseling functions may be included at those institutions which are committed to the use of correctional officers in the rehabilitation process.

Within the state correctional facilities, numerous employment possibilities exist beyond the correctional officer. These include the *living unit supervisor* (e.g., cottage parent), the various *industry shop supervisors*, those involved in *inmate reception and classification*, and a variety of special assignments related to counseling, the treatment program, and maintenance of the institution. In the latter case, the facility may be a farm, a lumber camp, or a unit assigned to road construction and repair. In such types of correctional units, the role of officer often doubles as *job supervisor* and *personal counselor.*

Later in this chapter, there is a list of the many opportunities and job titles which exist within this very extensive field of correctional custody, treatment, and rehabilitiation.

The following list of the correctional personnel categories demonstrates the variety of job opportunities existing within the field of corrections. This list is an excellent indication of the number of trained personnel required to effectively administer programs in the criminal justice field. Some of the workers serve at the beginning of the process, as in the case of gang workers in social agencies; some are employed as jail attendants in the pre-trial process; and others are utilized to administer the correctional system, either in institutions or as rehabilitation agents through the processes of probation and parole. As this system progresses toward the greater usage of non-institutional treatment-as well as a wider usage of small, minimum security-type institutions-the need for competent personnel enlarges. An individual considering a career choice should recognize that while these tasks vary insofar as immediate goals are concerned, all of them offer the opportunity to work with people in difficulty, and all, therefore, require sensitivity to human needs and a genuine interest in assisting one's fellow human beings.

JOB CATEGORIES
IN INSTITUTIONS

Administrators

Warden and Superintendent
Assistant/Associate Warden and
   Superintendent
Business Manager
Education Dept. Head
Line Correctional Staff Dept. Head
Director of Inmate Classification
Farm and Food Services Department
   Head
Maintenance Dept. Head
Prison Industries Superintendent
Director of Clinical/Treatment
   Services
Child Care Staff Dept. Head
Psychologist
Physical Education Teacher
Counselor
Institution Parole Officer

Line Workers

Cottage Parent/Counselor
Group Supervisor
Child Care Staff
Food and Farm Services
Maintenance
Prison Industries

JOB CATEGORIES IN PROBATION
AND PAROLE AGENCIES

Administrators

Director of Court Services
Chief Probation Officer/Director
Director of Parole Supervision
Assistant/Associate Chief Probation
   Officer/Director
District Director

Supervisors

Education Supervisor

Line Correctional Staff Supervisor
Prison Industries Shop and
   Factory Head
Child Care Staff Supervisor
Supervisor of Casework Services

Functional Specialists

Academic Teacher
Vocational Teacher or Instructor
Vocational and Educational Counselor
Classification Officer
Social Worker
Sociologist
Vocational Rehabilitiation Counselor

Supervisors

Staff Supervisor
District Supervisor
Assistant Supervisor

Functional Specialists

Field Probation Officer
Psychologist
Job Placement Officer
Field Parole Officer

OTHER CORRECTIONS
PERSONNEL

Chaplain
Attorney
Librarian
Medical and Dental personnel
Training Personnel
Research Personnel
Parole Board
Parole/Probation Aide
Business and Personnel Technical
   Assistant
Others as defined by the institution
   or agency

Specific career and job information may be obtained from the American Correctional Association; the American Probation & Parole Association; the Federal Bureau of Prisons; or the State Department of Corrections in the state of your own interest. For local facilities, one would contact the County Sheriff, city or county Department of Corrections, or the office of the county judge.

CRIMINALISTICS AND THE CRIME LAB

The career field that is perhaps most directly related to enforcement but that occurs in the laboratory and not on the street, is called *criminalistics* or forensic science. There are several paths into this scientific area, depending somewhat on the specialty. Most frequently, the criminalist is identified as someone who has majored in chemistry or physics and who has experience in applying this scientific competence to physical evidence and the questions of the criminal investigator.

The criminalist obtains experience through an internship while in college, and later, while employed in a crime laboratory. Because of the shortage of qualified persons in criminalistics, particularly those with graduate degrees, there are also opportunities to become a director of such a lab. Some criminalists prefer not to become involved in the administrative duties of a lab director, however, and therefore are employed as scientists engaged in the critical task of determining facts through their highly technical knowledge.

The *forensic scientist* is a more highly skilled and specialized scientific investigator in a single area of physical evidence analysis. As such, the forensic scientist generally is not as concerned with all physical/legal aspects of evidence as is the criminalist. The services of both are very important to enforcement agencies, as well as to the defense, and opportunities are always available for those who prepare for such careers through a background in the natural and physical sciences.

As with general enforcement work, there are laboratories at all jurisdictional levels. Some federal agencies have quite extensive facilities. Most notable, are those of the FBI, Drug Enforcement, and Post Office Departments. All states have lab facilities serving the headquarters of their state enforcement unit, in addition to other state labs that provide testing services primarily for the regulatory units in state government. Most of our major cities also have crime labs. Others, frequently known as regional forensic labs.

assist local departments in their entire region, so there are a number of locations for such employment.

In addition to the work of the chemist and physicist, there are lab-staffing needs in such fields as the polygraph (lie detector), the examination of questioned documents, fingerprint identification, and ballistics (firearms and tool identification), all of which require personal experience following considerable on-the-job training. Once the examiner is qualified as an expert, much of his or her time is spent testifying in courts. If one has a scientific and inquisitive mind, the work of the criminalist or laboratory-forensic examiner beckons.

The work of the criminalist or forensic scientist, whether a biologist, chemist, or physicist, consists of conducting tests related to a specialized area of science. The chemist may make determinations as to whether a stain is truly blood, whether a pill contains a narcotic drug, or whether a paint chipping came from a particular automobile fender. The physicist may make analyses of metals, glass, or other materials. Their primary concern in testing is to establish positive identifications and relationships to crimes, and their findings may determine a suspect's innocence or guilt.

Actually, most educational programs have the title "Forensic Sciences", and most of the crime laboratories today are given the label "Forensic Sciences". There is optimism about the job market for the forensic science specialist because recent surveys indicate that some 200 new people are needed each year. Since there are only some fourteen graduate programs nation-wide in Forensic Sciences, there continue to be vacancies for qualified individuals; salaries range from $20,000 to $30,000 for those with proper educational preparation and will be greater with experience and in the largest laboratories, such as the federal agency labs.

Forensic science therefore is a broad field in which physical and biological sciences are utilized to anaylze and evaualte physical evidence related to law. Physical evidence is any item of a physical state having the potential for providing information to the criminal justice system, civil litigation, or other matters of public interest and concern. Besides the criminalists, the forensic pathologists, and forensic toxicologists, these sciences include document examiners, anthropologists, psychiatrists, and a variety of chemists and others. Some departments and laboratories employ technicians who are skilled in certain instrumentation, but not necessarily in all aspects of the scientific profession. In preparation, one would normally follow a course of study through chemistry, instrumental analysis and microscopy, other sciences such as biology as they relate to evidence, and selected legal courses. For technican positions, one should complete as much high school math and science as possible and then look to more basic sciences in the community college. Many police lab technicians require only high school graduation and will encurage further study after employment. Positions such as Identification Technician provide excellent experience and training on-the-job in photography, evidence collection, preparing reports and classifying fingerprints, while permitting access to higher education as well.

Let us review some of the specialized examiners and scientists who are found within the forensic laboratory.

THE POLYGRAPH OPERATOR AND
THE DOCUMENT EXAMINER

The *polygraph operator*, or lie detector examiner, should have a working knowledge of human behavior and psychological responses. Through skillful testing of victims, suspects, witnesses, and others, this person is often able to determine whether or not an individual's verbal responses are truthful. The process of getting at totally truthful responses is a delicate one, and the examiner must have a sound knowledge of both personality differences and interviewing techniques. Again, and most importantly, the polygraph operator may determine one's *lack* of involvement in a particular criminal situation.

The *document examiner* has a variety of skills and tools with which to work. This specialist may be called on to analyze the signature on a check or compare known samples of a suspect's handwriting with a ransom note. In a more mechanical way, the document examiner may be asked to find out if a particular typewriter was used in the preparation of a deceased person's final will or whether the age of the ink and the age of the paper correspond on an alleged valuable document.

Document examiners deal with questions that need not always be criminal matters. One might be asked to help resolve cases involving the ages of conflicting or contested wills. Or one might be asked to resolve questions of signature authenticity in autographs, property deeds, and ownership titles.

FINGERPRINT AND FIREARMS EXPERT

The *expert in fingerprint identification* begins to obtain experience by classifying and comparing the many fingerprints on file in both criminal and non-criminal record systems. After considerable experience in making positive identifications and testifying to these in court, an examiner may become regarded as an expert. The importance of this means of identification cannot be overstressed, since it continues to this date to be our most positive single means of providing proof of individual identity. The expert in this field also will be called upon to make determinations in the case of footprints, palm prints, and other less common but equally positive sources.

The *firearms identification expert* is most frequently portrayed firing a revolver into a container and then making microscopic comparisons of the bullet in order to discover whether or not that particular weapon fired the suspect bullet. While such activities occupy some time, this specialist also is asked questions about whether a certain piece of metal came in contact with a specific door of a safe, or if a suspected burglary tool can positively be placed at the scene of a known break-in. The expert may also determine the distance that a shot was fired, the direction from which a bullet came, and what type of weapon was presumably used in a crime. The *firearms expert* deals with more than guns; all types of weapons and instruments are tested and compared.

Use of weapons on the firing range is a skill that law enforcment officers must master. State certification and academy requirements must be met. Photo: Miami-Dade Community College.

THE LAB TECHNICIAN

The increased demand in recent years for analysis of blood, drugs, and alcohol have highlighted the importance of a well-staffed laboratory. As has been pointed out by the Supreme Court, the police must rely more on scientifically determined physical evidence than on confessions.

In the crime laboratory, there are employment possibilities as a *laboratory technician*. The technician's specific duties would, of course, relate to the area of the lab in which he functions, and it is possible that, through continuing formal education and considerable on-the-job experience, the lab technician can become an examiner and ultimately, an expert in his field. Otherwise, there would be little potential for advancement in this highly specialized setting.

Outside of the laboratory, careers are emerging in the field of physical evidence. *Evidence technicians* are primarily responsible for the collection and packaging of all physical evidence at the crime scene and are expected to be proficient in the use of photographic equipment and in the making of sketches and plaster casts. The evidence technician, then, is responsible for the proper identification of suspicious items at the crime scene and for their safe delivery to the laboratory examiner.

More and more, lab work is being done through the use of mobile crime laboratories, and this in turn will demand more field personnel to inspect crime scenes, collect items for analysis, and perform necessary tests for later court presentation.

Some evidence technicians are police officers and some are civilians. The vehicles they use are equipped with everything from illumination devices, to facilities required to do field analyses of various kinds. They handle various photographic procedures, plaster and plastic casts, search out fingerprints and other forms of offender traces, operate a vacuum to collect hairs and fibers, and of course, must be able to collect and preserve properly any significant finding.

Forensic chemists, the most common of the laboratory professionals, are responsible for determining any connections that exist between case evidence and suspects. They conduct microscopic examinations and chemical tests on materials such as hair, fibres, skin, paint, glass, dirt, poisons, drugs, fabrics, gases, and substances of all types. Most of these tests, known as x-ray spectrometers, chromatography, ultra-violet and infrared spectrometers, and micro-photography, analyze unknown substances to determine and identify any significance to a crime. These chemists will be called upon to ascertain if a located sample is blood and if so, what type, and any other factors that can be indicated from that sample. Other body fluids can also be evaluated for positive linkages to offenders, victims, and suspects. Many new techniques have been introduced into the modern crime lab and precision instruments such as electronic cell counters, computers, and electronic microscopes demand both formal training and experience on-the-job. For one who has persistence, and not just patience, a talent for scientific inquiry, and a determination that can overcome the unpleasant odors, sights, and other frustrations, the employment outlook is quite favorable in the chemistry lab, and it is projected to continue to be so for the foreseeable future.

PRIVATE SECURITY AND LOSS PREVENTION

Yearly crime-related losses to the business and industrial community now total an estimated $22 billion. Retail business losses due to theft total $10 to $12 billion annually. There are over 12 million business and commercial establishments in the United States and only some 600,000 public police personnel to provide the needed protection and crime prevention.

The range of locations to be serviced runs from colleges to hotels; from airports to museums; from subway systems to financial institutions; and the requirements and rewards are just as varied. Many states have now enacted standards and training legislation and as these training requirements increase, so will the salaries. Presently an armed and trained private security officer can expect to earn between $800 and $1,200 per month. A medium-sized organization will pay $25,000-$30,000 for its Director of Security.

The national average for all private security directors today is $31,300. Highest director salaries are in utilities and manufacturing companies.

Recent studies indicate that over one million persons are employed within the framework of private industrial and retail security work. This can range from traditional *watchmen*, who are responsible for security in buildings and grounds, to *bank guards* and *railroad police* and can extend into more sophisticated assignments, such as *insurance investigation and loss prevention specialists*. Private security expenditures emphasize crime prevention through locks, alarms, patrol, TV surveillance, and other means of guarding persons and property.

In addition to the private security efforts of industry and business, there are numerous such employees who are assigned to specialized duties, but are on a public government payroll. This might include airport security personnel, college and university safety and security departments, the subway, tunnel, and harbor police. The 1977 Task Force Report on Private Security states that the private security system, with over one million workers, sophisticated alarm systems and perimeter safeguards, armored trucks, advanced mini-computers, and thousands of highly skilled crime prevention experts, offers a potential for coping with crime that cannot be equalled by any other remedy or approach.

Investigative careers also are offered by a number of commercial and private organizations which contract with firms or individuals for such services. Companies such as Pinkerton's National Detective Agency and Burns International Agency, and Wells Fargo, to name a few, are well-known to nearly everyone because of their uniformed guards, as well as notices on display in stores and on doors and windows. There are also a number of firms engaged in company protection, residence security, and private contract investigations. Salaries and advancement potential vary greatly in such work, and an applicant would be well-advised to first inquire as to the firm's reputation, since most states do have requirements set for obtaining private licenses.

Most major corporations and many businesses employ their own *security forces*. Employment therein usually is attractive and stable since such persons enjoy the benefits that accompany work in private industry. As concern over internal security, employee thefts, and inventory controls becomes more widespread, many companies are developing some fairly high-level, sophisticated, uniformed security units to provide safety and security within their own physical facilities.

Like public peace officers, these employees may be provided with some enforcement powers and may very likely possess communication equipment and weapons. Standards for such jobs are being raised, and the federal government has been encouraging the states to initiate minimum standards for entrance into retail and industrial security work.

As one might expect in the private sector, jobs at the top are competitive and well-rewarded. The proper combination of enforcement and investigative experience, coupled with higher education and some amount of management drive and skill, can lead one into a well-salaried position working for some particular company. Several former police chiefs from major cities serve as vice presidents for security and loss prevention with large corporations in the U.S., and their salaries exceed those earned while they were municipal police chiefs.

Private security forces now also have major responsibilities for safety and protection of many hospitals, schools, recreation facilities, public utilities, hotels, and financial institutions. The largest of these tend to be the manufacturing and retailing fields; health care and financial institutions are close behind.

Another large and growing employer is the shopping center and shopping mall itself where numbers of stores and businesses join together to purchase the contract services of a security firm, or perhaps, actually employ the officers themselves.

Department of Labor statistics for 1983 show that 23% of all employees in security-related fields are females. The private sector has a history of employing women in security work that predates by half a century that of the public police, since it was Alan Pinkerton who hired them as early as the 1850s.

It can be expected that private sector security will continue to increase and expand, to strengthen its standards, and increase its educational requirements. As computer theft becomes more common there will be even greater efforts to counter such crime and to employ persons with unique sets of skills. The future in this area is very good and one way to start is to obtain a uniformed officer security job while still a college student. Working part-time, on varied shifts, if even for minimum wage, is a way to start and obtain the necessary experience and reputation for dependability and resourcefulness. Even the college one is attending might have such employment available to students studying in criminal justice.

SUPPORTIVE JOBS

In addition to the aforementioned related careers, there is a variety of opportunities available for employment within enforcement agencies that can be referred to as supportive. In many departments, particularly the smaller ones, some of these may be performed by sworn personnel, but more and more, especially in large cities, they have become the responsibility of civilian personnel. Some of these services are related to *communications*, such as the receiving of incoming telephone calls, the dispatching of officers upon request, and obtaining complaints directly from citizens. Others relate to the immense *record-keeping* task, and included here are services related to accident reports, fingerprint classifications, criminal history files, and the routine processing of reports and case files.

Another major responsibility of any police agency is the *maintenance* of all property, and many hours are devoted to such items as evidence, lost and found items, property owned by prisoners, and even automobiles which have been impounded. Many departments employ *data analysts* who follow up on all reports submitted by officers and ensure their accuracy and proper completion. More recently, this function has involved dealing with computers and providing statistical data.

Civilians also may be involved in *public information, equipment maintenance, staff training, community relations, photography, jailer duties* in detention facilities, and such highly responsible duties as *comprehensive planning* and *computer analysis of crime data*. These jobs have been the result of the 1970's federal government initiatives in assisting local agencies by providing support for innovative and successful projects. A newly established career field, for example, is that of the planner in many agencies. Likewise, researchers and analysts will continue to be needed to assist with long range forecasting of needs and directions, and to assist decision makers through evaluation.

Earlier in this text we discussed the roles of community service officers, public service aides, and other non-sworn personnel. These positions, often involving taking complaints and reporting traffic problems and accidents, often appeal to persons who aspire to work in police departments but not as sworn officers. Of course, it is not uncommon for some public service officers to choose law enforcement as a career, particularly after they have pursued part or all of a college education.

Civilian positions may appeal to the young person interested in employment within the criminal justice system, but who is unable to meet certain specific physical or other qualifications for patrol duty. Or they may appeal to students who majored in business, economics, planning, computer science, physical sciences, information systems, or other disciplines that relate to but are not within the academic field that comprises the justice and safety systems. Civilian assignments also may be provided to former officers who are injured.

SUMMARY

A career in law enforcement is one of the most challenging in our complex modern society, and the demands made upon the law enforcement officer are so great that only those with excellent qualifications—physical, mental, and emotional—are selected. There is continuing community concern over the police problem today. The role of the police has changed in the eyes of the average citizen, and their peace-keeping and service-providing functions have become more apparent.

As the President's Crime Commission stated in the *Task Force Report* (on the) *Police* in 1967:

> The demands upon police are likely to increase in number and complexity in the years ahead, and dealing adequately with current law enforcement needs requires a clear acknowledgment that police are one of the most important governmental administrative agencies in evidence today.

Not only are the police an essential governmental agency, the makeup of enforcement personnel is even more important. As the National Advisory Commission on Criminal Justice Standards and Goals noted in 1973 regarding the needs of police personnel:

> The police service must recruit and employ the caliber of personnel that are now found within our colleges and universities, those possessing intellectual curiosity, analytical ability, articulateness, and a capacity to relate the events of the day to the social, political, and historical context in which they occur.

Young persons with an interest in working with people and in contributing their talents to improving our society will certainly find a career in law enforcement appropriate and satisfying. With the new era of the computer, with greater tactical flexibility, with a variety of new skills and techniques, as a modern peace officer today, you will be quite a contrast to your predecessors on the frontier. You will still be on the firing line, but now you will be armed with greater knowledge and with more supporting resources than ever before—yet to most citizens, you will still be the only contact with their government and its laws. Nothing can be more rewarding than to be instantly recognized by young and old alike as the guardian of peace, order, and justice—every hour, every day.*

---

*Every Hour, Every Day, movie produced by the International Association of Chiefs of Police, depicting careers and services rendered by modern police departments.

Physical conditioning is a crucial part of any law enforcement career and early morning runs are a regular part of the recruit's curriculum. Photo: Miami-Dade Community College.

In conclusion, a career in law enforcement can provide a rewarding opportunity for young men and women who believe that they would like to be in the most stimulating and unpredictable of the human service occupations. And, as in all other human services, the greatest rewards come in the form of personal satisfaction. No career can be more important to a democracy than one which protects all citizens in the community and is the recognized symbol of justice under our laws. But law enforcement is by no means an easy career; as we have tried to demonstrate, it is constantly changing to meet the new demands of a changing society. Today's peace officer faces challenges that cannot always be understood and which are not always able to be resolved. Many of these issues reach beyond the crime problem, yet they must be met immediately. If you feel confident that your personal qualifications are such that you could perform effectively a position of tremendous responsibility, you may want to consider a career in law enforcement or in one of the many related fields.

Jobs in law enforcement at all levels involve a great deal of paperwork. Photo: Safer Foundation.

CHAPTER 8

NATIONAL ASSOCIATIONS AND FEDERAL AGENCIES

There are a number of national organizations that provide information and materials to persons whose interests pertain to justice related careers. There are also a number of federal agencies which can provide career information directly and whose service also include publications and informational handouts.

Some of the national associations and organizations are listed below:

International Association of Chiefs of Police
13 Firstfield Road
Gaithersburg, MD 20878

This large membership organization provides training courses, written materials, and a variety of other services to its members and others. The Education and Training Committee serves as the vehicle to link the IACP with colleges, training academies and the resources being produced by commercial firms. A current listing of colleges and universities offering degree programs is available through IACP.

Academy of Criminal Justice Sciences
Secretariat
Center for Applied Urban Research
University of Nebraska
Omaha, NE 68182

Established in 1963 as the International Association of Police Professors, the Academy has broadened its base and changed its name. It is designed to futher communication and research among academic personnel concerned with the many issues involved in the criminal justice professions and their relationship with higher education. Student memberships are encouraged.

National Council on Crime & Delinquency
760 Market Street; #433
San Francisco, CA 94102

NCCD is a nonprofit citizen organization supported by contributions and foundations. It works to improve the criminal justice system and to maximize the effectiveness of all agencies within that system. It is especially concerned with stimulating community programs for the prevention, treatment and control of delinquency and crime.

National Sheriffs' Association
Suite 320
1250 Connecticut Avenue, N.W.
Washington D.C. 20036

NSA is a membership organization dedicated to furthering the goals of the Office of the Sheriff and the professional services which they represent. Career information may be available, as well as historical insights and current descriptive articles.

Lambda Alpha Epsilon
American Criminal Justice Association

Student/Alumni organization with a timely and informative Journal. Information about the organization and its purpose may be obtained from Virginia Commonwealth University; Administration of Justice & Public Safety Department; 901 W. Franklin Street; Richmond, VA 23284. Attn: Journal Editor, James E. Hooker.

This membership fraternity, formed in San Jose, California in 1937, welcomes pre-service students as well as those already employed in the justice field. Chapters are located across the country in colleges with active criminal justice education courses.

The national office, for membership inquiries, is Post Office Box 61047; Sacramento, CA 95860.

Others include:

International Association of Women Police
P.O. Box 7635, Kansas City, MO 64128

American Correctional Association .
Suite L-208, 4321 Hartwich Road, College Park, MD 20740

American Society of Criminology
1314 Kinnear Road; Suite 212
Columbus, OH 43212

American Society for Industrial Security
Suite 1200, 1655 No. Ft. Myer Drive
Arlington, VA 22209

Fraternal Order of Police
5613 Belair Road
Baltimore, MD 21206

Additionally, each state has its own Chiefs of Police Association, Sheriff's Association, and local chapters of the American Society for Industrial Security. There are also state chapters which are affiliates of the American Correctional Association in many states. All such organizations will attempt to provide employment assistance or career guidance if at all possible; some maintain a permanent staff for such services and others do not.

APPENDIX A

RECOMMENDED READINGS

JOURNALS

Corrections Today — American Correctional Association, 4321 Hartwick Road, Suite L-208, College Park, MD 20740

Crime & Delinquency — National Council on Crime & Delinquency, #433, 760 Market St., San Francisco, CA 94102

FBI Law Enforcement Bulletin — FBI, U.S. Department of Justice, Washington, D.C. 20535

Journal of Criminal Justice — Pergamon Press, Fairview Park, Elmsford, NY 10523

National Centurion — P.O. Box 27957, San Diego, CA 92128

National Sheriff — Suite 320, 1250 Connecticut Avenue, N.W., Washington, D.C. 20036

Journal of Police Science & Administration — IACP, 13 First Field Road, P.O. Box 6010, Gaithersburg, MD 20878

Police Studies — 444 West 56th Street, New York, NY 10019

Police Chief — International Association of Chiefs of Police, 13 Firstfield Road, P.O. Box 6010, Gaithersburg, MD 20878

Security World — Cahners Publishing Co., P.O. Box 5510, Denver, CO 80217

Security Management — American Society for Industrial Security, 1655 No. Ft. Myer Dr., Suite 1200, Arlington, VA 22209

Journal of Forensic Sciences — American Academy of Forensic Sciences, 225 So. Academy Blvd., Colorado Springs, CO 80910

Criminology — American Society of Criminology, 1314 Kinnear Road, Suite 212, Columbus, OH 43212

Alpha Phi Sigma Newsletter — Alpha Phi Sigma Law Enforcement Fraternity, c/o Texas Women's University, P.O. Box 23974—TWU Station, Denton, TX 76204

Journal of Security Administration — Academy of Security Educators & Trainers, 30 Falcon Drive, Hauppauge, NY 11788

International Criminal Police Review — ICPO — Interpol, 26 Rue Armengaud, 92210 Saint Cloud, France

Law and Order — 5526 Elston Avenue, Chicago, IL 60630

BOOKS

Abadinsky, H. *Probation & Parole,* Prentice Hall, Inc. 1982.

Baker, R. & Meyer, F. A. *Criminal Justice Game, Duxbury Press, North Scituate, Massachusetts, 1980.*

Bartollas, C., Miller, S. J., [Wice, P. B. *Participants in American Criminal Justice,* Prentice Hall, Inc., Englewood Cliffs, New Jersey, 1983.

Bristow, A. P. *Rural Law Enforcement,* Allyn & Bacon, Boston, Massachusetts, 1982.

Bopp, W. J. & Schultz, D. O. *Short History of American Law Enforcement,* Charles C. Thomas, Springfield, Illinois, 1977.

Elliott, J. F. *The New Police,* Charles C. Thomas, Springfield, Illinois, 1973.

Gallati, R. J. *Introduction to Private Security,* Prentice Hall, 1982.

Johnson, T., Misner, G. & Brown, L. *The Police & Society,* Prentice Hall, 1982.

Murphy, Patrick V. *Commissioner,* Simon & Schuster, New York, New York, 1977.

Niederhoffer, A. *The Police Family,* Lexington Books, D. C. Heath & Co., Boston, Massachusetts, 1978.

Pena, Manuel S. *Practical Police Criminal Investigation,* Custom Publishing Co., Costa Mesa, California, 1983.

Ricks, T. A., Tillett, B. G., & VanMeter, C. W. *Principles of Security,* Anderson Publishing Co., Cincinnati, Ohio, 1981.

Robin, Gerald D., *Introduction to the Criminal Justice System,* Harper & Row, New York, New York, 1983.

Scanlon, R. A. *Law Enforcement Bible No. 2,* Stoeger Publishing Co., South Hackensack, New Jersey, 1982.

Schultz, D. O. & Hunt, D. H. *Traffic Investigation & Enforcement,* Custom Publishing Co., Costa Mesa, California, 1983.

Swanson, C. R. & Chamelin, N. C. *Criminal Investigation,* Random House, New York, New York, 1981.

COLLEGES OFFERING CRIMINAL JUSTICE CURRICULA

Many community colleges and universities offer formal degree programs in criminal justice, and a large number of additional institutions of higher education offer criminal justice courses within other degree fields. Because of the recent acceleration of course and degree growth in this field, the following list is not meant to be all-inclusive, but represents institutions some of them known to have made a significant commitment to higher education and the criminal justice system in recent years.*

Alabama

    Jefferson St. Junior College
Birmingham 35215

    University of Alabama
Birmingham 35294

    Auburn University
Montgomery 36117

    Jacksonville State U.
Jacksonville 36265

    Troy State University
Troy 36081

Alaska

    Anchorage Comm College
Anchorage 99504

    University of Alaska
at Anchorage 99504

    Univ. of Alaska
Fairbanks 99701

    Northwest Comm College
Nome 99762

Arizona

    Arizona State University
Tempe 85281

Criminal Justice Education Directory 1980 Published and Distributed by International Association of Chiefs of Police.

Cochise College
Douglas 85607

Glendale Comm College
Glendale 85203

Mesa Comm College
Mesa 85202

Northern Arizona University
Flagstaff 86001

Phoenix College
Phoenix 85013

Pima Comm College
Tucson 85709

Scottsdale Comm College
Scottsdale 85251

Univ. of Arizona
Tucson 85721

Arkansas

Garland Co. Comm College
Hot Springs 71091

Univ. of Arkansas
Little Rock 72204

North Arkansas Comm College
Harrison 72601

California

Allan Hancock College
Santa Maria 93454

American River College
Placerville 95667

Antelope Valley College
Lancaster 93534

Bakersfield College
Bakersfield 93305

Barstow College
Barstow 92311

Butt Comm College
Oroville 95965

Cabrillo College
Aptos 95003

Calif. State College
San Bernardino 92407

Calif. State University
Fullerton 92634

Calif. State University
Fresco 93710

Calif. State University
Hayward 94542

Calif. State University
at Long Beach
Long Beach 90804

Calif. State University
at Los Angeles
Los Angeles 90032

Calif. State University
Sacramento 95819

Univ. of California
Berkeley 94720

Univ. of California
Irvine 92717

Cerritos College
Norwalk 90650

Chabot College
Hayward 94545

Chaffey College
Alta Loma 91701

Citrus College
Azusa 91702

Claremont Grad School
Claremont 91711

College of the Desert
Palm Desert 92260

College of the Redwoods
Eureka 95501

Compton College
Compton 90221

Contra Costa College
San Pablo 94806

De Anza College
Cupertino 95014

Diablo Valley College
Pleasant Hill 94523

East Los Angeles College
Los Angeles 90022

El Camino College
Torrance 90506

Fresno City College
Fresno 93741

Fresno State College
Fresno 93726

Fullerton College
Fullerton 92634

Gavilan College
Gilroy 95020

Glendale College
Glendale 91208

Golden West College
Huntington Beach 92647

Grossmont College
El Cajon 92020

Hartnell College
Salinas 93901

Imperial Valley College
Imperial 92251

Long Beach City College
Long Beach 90808

Los Angeles City College
Los Angeles 90029

Los Angeles Valley College
Van Nuys 91401

Marin, College of
Kentfield 94904

Merritt College
Oakland 94619

MiraCosta College
Oceanside 92054

Modesto Junior College
Modesto 95352

Monterey Peninsula College
Monterey 93940

Mount San Antonia College
Walnut 91789

Napa College
Napa 94558

Pasadena City College
Pasadena 91106

Pepperdine University
Los Angeles 90044

Peralta Colleges
Oakland 94609

Rio Hondo College
Whittier 90608

Riverside City College
Riverside 92506

Sacramento City College
Sacramento 95822

Saddleback College
Mission Viejo 92675

San Bernadino Valley College
San Bernadino 91786

San Diego Junior College
San Diego 92101

San Francisco, City College of
San Francisco 92101

San Joaquin Delta College
Stockton 95204

San Jose City College
San Jose 95114

San Jose State University
San Jose 95192

San Mateo, College of
San Mateo 94402

Santa Ana College
Santa Ana 92706

Santa Barbara City College
Santa Barbara 93109

Santa Monica City College
Santa Monica 90406

Santa Rosa Junior College
Santa Rosa 95401

Sequoias, College of the
Visalia 93277

Shasta College
Redding 96001

Sierra College
Rocklin 95677

Solano College
Vallejo 94590

Southern California, Univ. of
Los Angeles

Southwestern College
Chula Vista 92050

Ventura College
Ventura 93003

West Valley College
Campbell 95008

Yuba College
Marysville 95901

Colorado

Arapahoe Junior College
Littleton 80120

El Paso Comm College
Colorado Springs 80904

Metropolitan State College
Denver 80204

Trinidad State Junior College
Trinidad 81082

Connecticut

Eastern Connecticut State
College
Willimantic 06226

Manchester Comm College
Manchester 06040

New Haven University
West Haven 06516

Univ. of Connecticut
Storrs 06268

Norwalk Comm College
Norwalk 06854

University of Hartford
West Hartford 06117

Delaware

Brandywine College
Wilmington 19803

University of Delaware
Newark 19711

District of Columbia

American University
Washington, DC 20016

Washington Technical Institute
Washington, DC 20008

Florida

Biscayne College
Miami 33054

Brevard Junior College
Cocoa 32922

Broward Community College
Fort Lauderdale 33314

Central Florida Junior College
Ocala 32670

Chipola Comm College
Marianna 32446

Daytona Beach Comm College
Daytona 32015

Florida Atlantic Univ.
Boca Raton 33432

Florida International Univ.
Miami 33144

Florida Junior College at
Jacksonville
Jacksonville 32216

Florida Keys Community
College
Key West 33040

Florida State University
Tallahassee 32306

Florida Technological Univ.
Orlando 32816

Indian River Comm College
Ft. Pierce 33450

Lake City Comm College
Lake City 32055

Lake-Sumter Comm College
Leesburg 32748

Miami-Dade Comm College
Miami 33167

Palm Beach Junior College
Lake Worth 33460

Pensacola Junior College
Pensacola 32504

St. Petersburg Junior College
St. Petersburg 33733

Tallahassee Junior College
Tallahassee 32303

Valencia Junior College
Orlando 32802

Univ. of Tampa
Tampa 33606

Univ. of North Fl.
Jacksonville 32216

Univ. of South Florida
Tampa 33620

*North Fl. Comm College
Madison 32340

*Santa Fe Comm College
Gainesville 32601

Georgia State University
Atlanta 30303

Georgia, University of
Athens 30601

Kennesaw Junior College
Marietta 30060

Valdosta State College
Valdosta 31601

Hawaii

Honolulu Comm College
Honolulu 96817

Idaho

Boise College
Boise 83707

College of Southern Idaho
Twin Falls 83301

Illinois

Black Hawk College
Moline 61265

Carl Sandburg College
Galesburg 61401

College of Dupage
Naperville 60540

Danville Junior College
Danville 61832

Illinois Central College
East Peoria 61611

Joliet Junior College
Joliet 60432

Chicago City-wide College
Chicago 60601

Prairie State College
Chicago Heights 60411

Rock Valley College
Rockford 61111

Sangamon State Univ.
Springfield 62708

Southern Illinois Univ.
Carbondale 62901

Triton College
River Grove 60171

Richard J. Daley College
Chicago 60652

Saint Xavier College
Chicago 60655

University of Illinois at
Chicago Circle
Chicago 60680

Wabash Valley College
Mt. Carmel 52863

Waubonsee Comm College
Sugar Grove 60554

Western Illinois University
Macomb 61455

William Rainey Harper College
Palatine 60067

Indiana

Ball State University
Muncie 47306

Indiana Central University
Indianapolis 46227

Indiana State University
Terre Haute 47803

Indiana University
Bloomington 47401

University of Evansville
Evansville 47704

Vincennes University
Vincennes 47591

Iowa

Des Moines Comm College
Ankeny 50021

Iowa Central Comm College
Fort Dodge 50501

Iowa Western Comm College
Clarinda 51632

Kirkwood Comm College
Cedar Rapids 52406

North Iowa Comm College
Cedar Rapids 52406

Southeastern Comm College
W. Burlington 52601

State University of Iowa
Iowa City 52240

University of Iowa
Iowa City 52240

Kansas

Allen County Comm College
Iola 66749

Butler Co. Comm College
El Dorado 67042

Colby Comm College
Colby 67701

Cowley County Comm College
Arkansas City 67005

Garden City Comm College
Garden City 67846

Hutchinson Comm Junior
College
Hutchinson 67501

Kansas City Comm College
Kansas City 66112

Washburn University
Topeka 66621

Wichita State University
Wichita 67208

Kentucky

Eastern Kentucky Univ.
Richmond 40475

Murray State University
Murray 42071

Paducah Comm College
Paducah 42001

University of Louisville
Louisville 40208

Louisiana

Louisiana State University
Baton Rouge 70803

Loyola University
New Orleans 70118

McNeese State University
Lake Charles 70601

Northeast Louisiana Univ.
Monroe 71209

Southeastern Louisiana Univ.
Hammond 70402

Maine

University of Maine
August 04330

University of Maine
Bangor 04401

University of Maine
Portland 04103

Maryland

Ann Arundel Comm College
Arnold 21012

Catonsville Comm College
Catonsville 21228

Cecil Comm College
Elkton 21921

Comm College of Baltimore
Baltimore 21215

Essex Comm College
Essex 21221

Frederick Comm College
Frederick 21701

Hagerstown Junior College
Hagerstown 21740

Harford Comm College
Bel Air 21014

Montgomery College
Rockville 20850

Prince George's Comm College
Largo 20810

University of Baltimore
Baltimore 21201

University of Maryland
College Park 20742

Massachusetts

Bristol Comm College
Fall River 02720

Cape Cod Comm College
West Barnstable 02668

Dean Jr. College
Franklin 02038

Greenfield Comm College
Greenfield 01301

Holyoke Comm College
Holyoke 01040

Massasoit Comm College
Brockton 02402

Mount Wachusett Comm
College
Gardner 01440

North Shore Comm College
Beverly 01915

Northeastern University
Boston 02115

Quinsigamond Comm College
Worcester 01606

University of Lowell
Lowell 01854

Worcester Junior College
Worcester 01608

Michigan

Delta College
University Center 48710

Eastern Michigan University
Ypsilanti 48197

Fling Comm Junior College
Flint 48503

Glen Oaks Comm College
Centreville 49032

Grand Rapids Junior College
Grand Rapids 49502

Jackson Comm College
Jackson 49201

Kellogg Comm College
Battle Creek 49016

Lansing Comm College
Lansing 48914

Macomb County Comm College
Mt. Clemens 48043

Mercy College of Detroit
Detroit 48219

Michigan State University
East Lansing 48823

Muskegon Comm College
Muskegon 49443

Northern Michigan University
Marquette 49855

Oakland Comm College
Oakland 48104

St. Clair County Comm College
Port Huron 48060

Schoolcraft College
Livonia 48151

Wayne State University
Detroit 48202

Western Michigan University
Kalamazoo 49008

Minnesota

Lakewood Comm College
St. Paul 55110

Bemidju State University
Bemidji 56601

Rochester Comm College
Rochester 55901

University of Minnesota
Duluth 55812

Metropolitan Comm College
Minneapolis 55403

St. Cloud State College
St. Cloud 56301

University of Minnesota
Minneapolis 55455

Mississippi

Gulf Coast Jr. College
Gulfport 39501

Mississippi State Univ.
Mississippi State 39762

University of Mississippi
University 38677

Univ. of Southern Mississippi
Hattiesburg 39401

Wm. Carey College
Hattiesburg 39401

Missouri

Central Missouri State College
Warrensburg 64093

Florissant Valley Comm College
St. Louis 63135

Forest Park Comm College
St. Louis 63110

Meramee Comm College
Kirkwood 63137

Missouri Southern College
Joplin 64801

Missouri Western St. College
St. Joseph 64507

Northeast Missouri St.
University
Kirksville 63501

Penn Valley Comm College
Kansas City 64111

Southeast Missouri St.
University
Cape Girardeau 63701

University of Missouri
Kansas City 64110

University of Missouri
St. Louis 63121

Montana

College of Great Falls
Great Falls 59405

Dawson College
Glendive 59330

University of Montana
Missoula 59812

Montana State University
Bozeman 53715

Nebraska

Kearney State College
Kearney 68847

University of Nebraska
Lincoln 68508

Metropolitan Comm College
Omaha 68137

University of Nebraska
Omaha 68101

Nevada

Nevada Technical Institute
Reno 98507

Northern Nevade Comm
College
Elko 89801

University of Nevada
Las Vegas 89154

Western Nevada Comm College
Carson City 89701

New Hampshire

New Hampshire Voc-Tech
College
Portsmouth 03801

St. Anselms College
Manchester 03102

New Jersey

Atlantic Comm College
May's Landing 08330

Burlington County College
Pemberton 08068

Camden County College
Blackwood 08012

Essex County College
Newark 07102

Glassboro State College
Glassboro 08028

Jersey City State College
Jersey City 07305

Mercer County Comm College
Trenton 08690

Middlesex County College
Edison 08817

Ocean County College
Tom's River 08753

Patterson College of NJ
Wayne 07470

Rider College
Trenton 08602

Rutgers, The State University
New Brunswick 08903

Trenton State College
Trenton 08625

New Mexico

Eastern New Mexico St.
University
Clovis 88101

New Mexico St. University
Las Cruces 88001

University of Albuquerque
Albuquerque

New York

Auburn Comm College
Auburn 13021

Clinton Comm College
Plattsburg 12901

Dutchess Comm College
Poughkeepsie 12601

Elmira College
Elmira 14901

Erie Community College
Buffalo 14221

Hudson Valley Comm College
Troy 12180

Jamestown Comm College
Jamestown 14701

Jefferson Comm College
Watertown 13601

John Jay College of Criminal
Justice
New York 10019

Long Island University
Brooklyn 11201

Mercy College
Dobbs Ferry 10522

Mohawk Valley Comm College
Utica 13501

Monroe Comm College
Rochester 14623

Nassau Comm College
Garden City 11530

New York Inst. of Technology
Old Westbury 11568

New York State University
Farmingdale, L.I. 11735

New York University
New York 10003

Onondaga Comm College
Syracuse 13210

Orange County Comm College
Middletown 10940

Rochester Institute of
Technology
Rochester 14623

Rockland Comm College
Suffern 10901

Russell Sage College
Troy 12180

State Univ. of New York
Albany 12222

Suffolk County Comm College
Seldon, L.I. 11784

State University of NY
Buffalo 14222
Brockport 14420
Canton 13617
Stony Brook 11794
Utica/Rome 13502

Ulster County Comm College
Stone Ridge 12484

Westchester Comm College
Valhalla 10595

North Carolina

Appalachian State Univ.
Boone 28608

Central Piedmont Comm
College
Charlotte 28204

Davidson Comm College
Lexington 27292

Durham Technical Institute
Durham 27703

East Carolina University
Greenville 27834

Fayetteville State Univ.
Fayetteville 28301

Forsyth Technical Institute
Winston-Salem 27102

Gaston College
Sylva 28779

Martin Comm College
Williamson 27892

Roanoke-Chowan Tech Institute
Ahoskie 27910

Rowan Tech Institute
Salisbury 28144

Southwestern Technical Institute
Sylva 28779

Surry Comm College
Dobson 27017

Vance-Granville Comm College
Henderson 27536

Western Carolina University
Cullowhee 28723

University of North Carolina
Charlotte 28213

Wilson City Technical Institute
Wilson 27893

North Dakota

Bismarck Jr. College
Bismarck 58501

Univ. of North Dakota
Grand Fork 58201

Minot State College
Minot 58701

Ohio

Clark County Technical
Institute
Springfield

Cuyahoga Comm College
Cleveland 44115

Hocking Technical Institute
Nelsonville 45764

Kent State University
Kent 44240

Lakeland Comm College
Mentor 44060

Lorain County Comm College
Elyria 44035

Owens Technical College
Perrysburg 43551

Sinclair Comm College
Dayton 45402

University of Akron
Akron 44325

University of Cincinnati
Cincinnati 45221

University of Dayton
Dayton 45409

University of Toledo
Toledo 43606

Youngstown State Univ.
Youngstown 44503

Xavier University
Cincinnati 45207

Oklahoma

Central State University
Edmond 73034

Northern Oklahoma College
Tonkawa 74653

Oklahoma City University
Oklahoma City 73106

Oklahoma State University
Stillwater 74074

Seminole Jr. College
Seminole 74868

Tulsa Jr. College
Tulsa 74119

University of Oklahoma
Norman 73019

University of Tulsa
Tulsa 74104

Oregon

Blue Mountain Comm College
Pendleteon 97801

Clackamas Comm College
Oregon City 97045

Clatsop Comm College
Astoria 97103

Lane Comm College
Eugene 97405

Lima Benton Comm College
Albany 97321

Portland Comm College
Portland 97219

Portland State University
Ashland 97207

Rogue Comm College
Grants Pass 97526

Southern Oregon College
Ashland 97520

Treasure Valley Comm
Ontario 97914

Umpqua Comm College
Roseburg 97470

Pennsylvania

Bucks County Comm College
Newtown 18940

Butler County Comm College
Butler 16001

Comm College of Allegheny
County
Monroeville 15146

Comm College of Beaver
County
Monaca 15061

Comm College of Philadelphia
Philadelphia 19107

Edinboro State College
Edinboro 16444

Harrisburg Area Comm College
Harrisburg 17110

Kings' College Wilkes
Barre 18711

Indiana Univ. of Pennsylvania
Indiana 15701

Lehigh County Comm College
Schnecksville 18078

Luzerme County Comm College
Nanticoke 18634

Mansfield State College
Mansfield 16933

Mercyhurst College
Erie 16501

Montgomery County Comm
College
Blue Bell 19422

Pennsylvania State Univ.
University Park 16802

University of Pittsburgh
Pittsburgh 15260

University of Scranton
Scranton 18510

Temple University
Philadelphia 19122

York College
York 17405

Rhode Island

Bryant College
Providence 02906

The Newport College
Newport 02840

Roger Williams College
Bristol 02809

South Carolina

Beaufort Technical College
Beaufort 29902

Greenville Technical Education Center
Greenville 29606

Spartanburg Junior College
Spartanburg 29301

Piedmont Tech College
Greenwood 29646

Trident Technical College
Charleston 29401

University of South Carolina
Columbia 29208

South Dakota

Black Hills State College
Spearfish 57783

Huron College
Huron 57350

Northern State College
Aberdeen 57401

University of South Dakota
Vermillion 57069

Tennessee

Cleveland State Comm College
Cleveland 37311

East Tennessee State Univ.
Johnson City 37601

Memphis State University
Memphis 38152

Middle Tennessee State Univ.
Murfreesboro 37150

Shelby State Comm College
Memphis 38104

Texas

Amarillo College
Amarilo 79178

American Technological University
Killeen 76541

Central Texas College
Killeen 76541

College of the Mainland
Texas City 77590

Del Mar College
Corpus Christi 78404

East Texas State Univ.
Commerce 75428

El Centro College-of the Dallas City Jr. College District
Dallas 75202

El Paso Comm College
El Paso 79904

Galveston College
Galveston 77550

Grayson County Jr. College
Denison 75020

Lee College
Baytown 77520

McLennan Comm College
Waco 76708

Midwestern State Univ.
Wichita Falls 76306

Odessa College
Odessa 79760

Pan American University
Edinburg 78539

Sam Houston State Univ.
Huntsville 77340

San Antonio College
San Antonio 78212

San Jacinto College
Pasadena 77501

South Texas Junior College
Houston 77002

Southwest Texas State Univ.
San Marcos 78666

Stephen F. Austin State Univ.
Nacagooches 75962

Tarrant County Jr. College
Hurst 76053

Texarkana Comm College
Texarkana 75501

Texas Eastern University
Tyler 75701

University of Houston
Houston 77058

University of Texas
Arlington 76019

Utah

Brigham Young University
Provo 84602

Southern Utah State College
Cedar City 84720

Weber State College
Ogden 84408

Vermont

Castleton State College
Castleton 05735

Virginia

Blue Ridge Comm College
Weyers Cave 24486

Central Virginia Comm College
Lynchburg 24502

D. S. Lancaster Comm College
Clifton Forge 24422

Danville Comm College
Danville 24541

J. Sargeant Reynolds Comm
College
Richmond 23241

John Tyler Comm College
Chester 23821

New River Comm College
Dublin 24084

Northern VA Comm College
Annandale 22003
Manassas 22110
Woodbridge 22191

Paul D. Camp Comm College
Franklin 23851

Piedmont Virginia Comm
College
Charlottesville 22903

Southside Virginia Comm
College
Keysville 23947

Thomas Nelson Comm College
Hampton 23670

Tidewater Comm College
Virginia Beach 23451

Virginia Commonwealth Univ.
Richmond 23284

VA Highlands Comm College
Abingdon 24210

Virginia Western Comm College
Roanoke 24015

Washington

Bellevue Comm College
Bellevue 98004

Central Wash-State College
Ellensburg

City College
Seattle 98020

Clark College
Vancouver 98663

Eastern University
Cheney 99004

Everett Comm College
Everett 98201

Fort Steilacoom Comm College
Tacoma 98499

Green River Comm College
Auburn 98002

Highline Comm College
Midway 98031

North Seattle Comm College
Seattle 98103

Olympic College
Bremerton 98310

Pacific Lutheran Univ.
Tacoma 98447

Pacific Western College
Renton 98055

Seattle University
Seattle 98122

Shoreline Comm College
Seattle 98133

Spokane Community College
Spokane 99202

Tacoma Comm College
Tacoma 98465

Washington State Univ.
Pullman 99164

Yakima Valley College
Yakima 98902

West Virginia

Bluefield State College
Bluefield 24701

Marshall University
Huntington 25701

Fairmont State College
Fairmont 26554

Parkersburg Comm College
Parkersburg 26101

Salem College
Salem 26426

Southern West Virginia
   Community College
Logan 25601

West Liberty State College
West Liberty 26074

West Virginia Northern Comm
   College
Wheeling 26003

West Virginia State College
Institute 25112

Wisconsin

Blackhawk Tech. Institute
Beloit 53511

Dist. One Tech. Institute
Eau Claire 54701

Kenosha Technical Institute
Kenosha 53140

Madison Area Technical
   College
Madison 53703

Marquette University
Milwaukee 53233

Mid-State Technical Inst.
Wisconsin Rapids 54494

Milwaukee Area Technical
   College
Milwaukee 53203

North Central Tech. Institute
Wausau 54401

North East Tech. Institute
Green Bay 54303

University of Wisconsin
Milwaukee 53201

Wisconsin State University
Platteville 53818

Wyoming

Casper College
Casper 82601

Laramie County Comm College
Cheyenne 82001

Sheridan College
Sheridan 82801

University of Wyoming
Laramie 82070

U.S. Outlying Possessions

Guam

University of Guam
Agana 96910

Virgin Islands

College of the Virgin Islands
St. Thomas 00801

Inter-American Univ. of
Puerto Rico
San Juan 00936

11484   18,653

DATE			
MAY 1 4 1992			
MAR 3 1999			
MAR 2 0 2000			
6 2002			
JUN 3 2002			
PR 6 '04			